THE
HEART
of the *Family*

THE
HEART
of the Family

Italian Immigrant Women
in Mining Communities: 1880–1920

PHYLIS CANCILLA MARTINELLI, PHD

MILL CITY PRESS

Mill City Press, Inc.
2301 Lucien Way #415
Maitland, FL 32751
407.339.4217
www.millcitypress.net

Paperback ISBN-13: 978-1-6628-5245-9
Ebook ISBN-13: 978-1-6628-5246-6

Dedication

To Philip Anthony Martinelli my husband of over 55 years,
His encouragement about the need to publish
this book moved me forward.

CHAPTER 1

Transition: From Farming to Mining to Industry

The Industrial Revolution

The need for mining copper and coal in the United States dates back to the industrial Revolution that originated in England, about 1775 until 1848. The European economy gradually moved from for almost all work done by humans or animals work, to machines and mechanical labor.

One key invention was made by James Watt who invented a reliable steam engine that began to serve a variety of purposes. Farming too changed, crop rotation became common. More sophisticated farming methods needed less workers and resulting exodus of surplus labor led to migration at first to cities and later to other parts of the world. In 1839 Englishman Francis Pettit Smith pioneered the first propeller driven ship for naval use; later commercial ships were built. These would eventually replace older wooden sail driven ships and allowed for the movement of thousands of people to the United States from Europe.

The Industrial Revolution rocked Europe over a century ago, bringing dramatic changes in the areas of transportation, religion, industry, healthcare, population trends, urbanization, education, and intellectual trends. New inventions, like the use of steam power, revolutionized lives. Birth rates began to soar as scientific knowledge about healthcare grew. It was finally realized that conditions during childbirth needed to be sanitary. For the first time, those helping with a birth washed their hands before the delivery. This meant that women were no longer dying of "child bed fever" or puerperal infections after child birth. With women living extended lives and their infants were doing better, overpopulation became a pressing social issue.

At the same time, the Catholic Church's influence was waning, as the Protestant faith grew. Unfortunately, an effective method of birth control, besides abortion or abstinence, had yet to be discovered. Some men still saw having numerous children as a sign of virility. Although subsistence agriculture was in decline, having many children was still considered a blessing because it meant more hands to work the land.

The initial nations that benefited from modernization were England and Northern Europe. Mediterranean nations such as Greece and Italy were slower to industrialize hence their populations migrated at a different time than Northern Europeans did. This book tells the story of migrants from Northern Italy, women who migrated to the United States to work in mining camps in the newly very important industries of coal and copper mining. I doubt that this inexpensive and disposable labor force would have made the impact it did except for the women who came to start or maintain families provided a settled environment for the men who did the labor. These Northern Italian women became the heart of the families in many mining camps.

Like Elizabeth Scott[1] who championed those overlooked groups or 'those of little note' whose presence in archaeology is often not commented on due to their low status related to their gender, ethnicity or class, my interest is on the lives of poor immigrant women from Italy.

In the old mining towns of the U.S. West, the mining companies provided the housing, but the women provided "the home." It was up to women to transform the dilapidated housing furnished by the company into a true home. The very presence of women in the mining camps made life more tolerable for the miners. What was the difference between housing and a home for a newly arrived immigrant? This book examines the lives of Italian immigrant women in mining communities from 1870-1930. The impact of living conditions, housing, company practices, discrimination, and unions influence on life in the mining camps is also discussed. In certain academic circles, the story of Rosa Cavalleri, an Italian immigrant from Lombardia in Northern Italy, who spent some time in an iron mining camp in Missouri, is well-known. Rosa's story was recounted to a social worker who wrote an in-depth and well-recognized biography of this immigrant woman's experiences.[2] The account of Rosa's life is well worth reading! For the purposes of this book, however, I am highlighting the brave, hard-working, determined Italian immigrant women who have been forgotten by history as those of little note. Their stories deserve to be told as well.

The "first wave" of immigration to the United States was from Northern Europe and included many already skilled in mining, such as the Cornish and Germans. These people were Protestant and were considered "white." Irish Catholics were outside the norm due to their religious preferences, Catholics were believed, by some, to be loyal only to the Pope. Those in the "second wave" were Eastern Europeans from eastern nations such as central Europe, like Poland, and Mediterranean nations, such as Italy, Greece, and Spain. Most were not Protestant but Catholic, Orthodox (Greek), or Jewish. Their "whiteness" was called into question by the Anglo-Saxon settlers already in the States who claimed whiteness as their own. Italian immigrants were the largest group to go into mining during the "second wave" of European immigration to the United States according to Foerster.[3] In the

United States, as the demand for both coal and copper greatly increased during the Civil War more workers were needed.[4]

Mining companies began to build small homes on small parcels of land. Hence, miners began to refer to their neighborhoods as a patch. Italian migrants from Tyrol referred to housing in mining towns as "patches,"[5] Usually, workers rented their homes. They did not own the land. This allowed a company to evict a family if the husband went on strike; it was a covert means of social control.

Companies provided housing for mining sites, not out of largess, but due to necessity. Most ores were found in remote areas where housing was not readily available. Additionally, providing housing benefited a company because it kept workers dependent upon the employer. In many cases married men migrated alone. If they found a place that suited them, they would bring their wives and families to the new country. Of course, not all did this. Some would return home to find a suitable bride. Others, through an arranged marriage, were able to find a woman willing to travel from Italy to marry them.

In the late 1800s and early 1900s, Italian women lived in a highly patriarchal society. They had very little legal or official status. Once married, everything that belonged to a woman was transferred her husband. In Italy, women were not given the right to vote until 1946. Thus, women were left with little economic or political power according to *the Instituto Italiano di Culture,*[6] Within the family however, women had greater influence. According to an Italian saying, in public "the man is the head of the household," yet within the home "the woman is the heart of the family." As Donna Gabaccia notes that once a woman married she would control the family's purchases as well as arrange marriages for the children "in this way women exercise considerable family influence. Mothers became the emotional centers of their immediate families."[7] Much of this book is based on oral histories or contemporary accounts from the daughters of Italian immigrant women who lived in mining camps.

Another inspiration for me is Illaria Serra's book which shows the effect of these women on both the social and psychological adjustments of immigrants. Illaria Serra too stresses the importance of seemingly inconsequential lives; the title of her book, says it all: *The Value of Worthless Lives.*[28] Her ideas about the importance of oral histories and biographic local expressions can to be seen as part of our current Information age where new technology and a growing emphasis on self-expression may encourage some of the newest immigrants to the United States to recount their lives. All of them can be can be added to the tapestry that is part of modern society as we continue to see the arrival of new immigrants and refugees.

Historian Dorothy Schwieder[9], whose work on *Iowa* is an important source for this book, recounts the history of coal mining through oral histories of immigrants both men and women and their children. For the coal mining town of Thurber, Texas, I do not have oral histories due to the company's desire to distance outsiders from the miners. In most books on Thurber, Italian immigrants and their wives are mentioned as part of the multi-ethnic makeup of the camp. Specifics on women are scant, although I did find a few references to the lives of women from some books on the town and state. Victor Lucadello, wrote about his mother, and Mauro Toniutti, wrote about his great grandmother. For copper mining families in company housing Upper Michigan (U. P.) was, in many ways, more benevolent than the coal mining companies. For the section on the U.P., oral histories were done by a graduate student, Sara Rice, who made her work available to me. My own research on Italian women in the copper mining town of Globe, Arizona completes this part of this book.

CHAPTER 2

Migration from Italy

Map of pre-unification Italy

Any marketing company would have a difficult time coming up with a more recognizable logo for Italy than the" boot". Unfortunately, during the years before the great Italian migration to America, this "boot" more closely resembled a jig-saw puzzle of a boot than one you could slip on your foot. In this chapter, I explore the political, economic, and social factors that led to Italian migration to the New World. I then focus on the racial tensions faced by many Italians both in their own country and after they crossed the Atlantic. Centuries had passed since the decline of the Roman Empire and now Italy was in fragments.

The puzzle pieces: From 1701 onward, the Austro-Hungarian Empire controlled much of Northeastern Italy. At the same time, the center of Italy was controlled by the Papal States; the Papal control extended far beyond Rome. Starting in 1717, Spain controlled Southern Italy by the Kingdom of the Two Sicilies. The Kingdom of Sardinia occupied both the Island of Sardinia and the Piedmont-Savoy region of Italy in the North.

Italy Unifies

As Europe changed with the Industrial Revolution, France was also struggling to modernize. Part of this effort involved sending French forces to crush interference from other nations. In a successful move against the Austrians, French troops pushed Austria out of northeastern Italy. As leader of the army, Napoleon's personal reputation and wealth were rapidly growing. He was quick to carve up Italy and enrich his troops with spoils from conquered areas; he declared himself Emperor of Italy in 1805. By doing so, he inadvertently planted seeds for a new, unified Italy. Nine years later, he was forced out of Italy.[10]

The unification of Italy began in 1830 ended in 1871. (These dates vary depending on whom you read.) Chief among those pushing for change was the young Giuseppe Mazzinni, whose name is often associated with the *risorgimento,* or in English renewal. Giuseppe Garibaldi agreed with these new ideas, and, with his Red Shirt Army, gained the southern area for the United Kingdom of Italy. Victor Emmanuel II of Sardinia was proclaimed King of a unified Italy in 1861, a title he held till his death. [11]

Ironically, this period of unification saw a major exodus from the peninsula to other parts of Europe and the Americas. Italy had no common language. Many regions spoke their own local dialect or Austrian. In the former Austrian area of Italy, in Bolzano, a form of German was spoken still in the 1970s. Throughout the newly unified Italy, a form of official Latin was used for business. A national language failed to edge out local dialects until fairly recently.

Italy's unification had little positive impact on the lives of peasants. If a period of despotism was needed in order to form a unified nation, so be it. [12] Because of the political unrest of this time, we see the first wave of migration from the North of Italy— departing through the ports of Genoa and Venice. Northern Italy consisted roughly of the area above Rome. Only through migration was the dramatic population surge in Italy diminished.

Northern Italy

Following the unification of Italy, Northern Italians left for other parts of Europe and the Americas after years of enduring privation and political unrest. In some parts of the province of Piemonte a system of land tenure, "primogeniture," by which the eldest son inherited everything, meant that younger sons, having few options other than a religious vocation or joining the military, often tried emigration. The system of primogeniture drove my maternal grandfather to the United States. In the North, the wealthy held most of the land—and most of the "good" land. A poor farmer had little hope of ever gaining such land. Many farmed small acreages, while some women did seasonal work in the silk industry. Many Piemontese in U.S. mining towns came from the rocky areas above Torino, capital of the province.

Southern Italy

Migration from Southern Italy began in earnest between 1900 and 1914 as people fled unbelievable *miseria* (poverty). They, like their northern neighbors, longed for a better life for themselves and the children. My Sicilian

9

family shared stories of the poverty they faced before they came to America. Work opportunities in the New Continent were attractive, as were the prospects of education and political freedom.[13] As three-fourths of the Italian immigrants to the United States were from the South of Italy, the image of Italians, in the mind of many Americans, was of Southern Italians. Unfortunately, this image was not always positive. Some negative stereotypes still persist. I was reassured that no one in our family had any connections with the Mafia. Due to the overwhelming numbers of Southern Italians who migrated to the U.S., the culture of Northern Italians has been overlooked by most Americans. In time, Northerners would become invisible, as would most of their culture.

Life of a Northern Peasant Farmer

Lorenzo Sartore,[14] a miner in the United States described the life of in his family in Italy. "My father was a farmer. He, together with my mother, I remember used to work very hard leaving the house very early in the morning with a four wheeled cart drawn by two oxen. My father in front of them steering them along with a stick leading them onto the field to do the seeding and planting of wheat, corn, etc. My mother following in the back of the cart with a rake on her shoulder was going to help my father. They worked very hard all day. The only time for rest was under a shady tree to eat their meager lunches, they never return home until dark, very tired. At the day work was not yet finished for them. We had in the stable with from 6 to 8 milk cows and some calf. My mother used to prepare supper for us all, my father had to feed the cows, milk the cows and clean the stable. By this time my mother had supper ready for us. We all sat and eat supper together. After supper we used to gather all of us in the stable especially in the winter months. Lorenzo noted that the stable with all the animals was warm, and the only means we had to keep warm in the winter around the stable there were benches for myself and my brothers and sisters used to sit and spend the time. My mother had a spinning wheel she used to make yarn. With this yarn she made bed sheets, towels and other linen necessary for us. Before going to bed my mother used to gather all of us together and used to recite the rosary altogether. My mother was a very religious person, a beautiful person. May God bless her." Unlike farmers in the United States who tended to have several acres of land, Italian farmers often had only a small plot of land and grew subsistence crops there. While they might raise a few chickens and pigs on their land there was not room for enough cows to make a good profit. The small amount of money father could gain from his crops and dairy products did not lift them out of poverty.

North vs. South

How did the two regions differ? One subtle difference was seen in family structure. According to Foerster the physical environment influenced the way in which families formed.[15] Northern Italy, especially Piemonte and Lombardia, had water from the Alps, which was brought to farms by a complex system of canals. In addition, northern Italy has several major rivers. Beginning in 1220, the people of Lodi, Lombardia, were able to construct miles of artificial rivers and channels, making this region more fertile.[16] Those crops, like rice, that require a lot of water grow best in northern Italy. There, extended families had land to farm together. In addition the fertile plains of northern Italy draw on the Po River, which is the largest in Italy. In contrast, Southern families were smaller, nuclear families because they faced land fragmentation due to deforestation and the lack of a major river as a reliable water source.

In the North, during the Industrial Age, the attitude towards work changed as people were exposed to the contemporary idea of working for someone else. The first Italian industries developed in Northern Italy. As working for someone else in factories meant following a strict time schedule, by the time Northerners migrated to the U.S., they were accustomed to scheduled workdays. As Southern Italy was further from Northern Europe, Italians from the South were used to the more relaxed schedules of farmers.

There were other significant differences between Northern and Southern Italy, such as education. For instance, education was more readily available in the North and both men and women could read and write in the dialect of their region. In the South, however, education was almost nonexistent for peasants. Although Northerners were viewed as anticlerical, both regions celebrated Saints' Days. In the North, Saint John's Day was important, while in the South, the feast day of St. Joseph was important, especially in Sicily. Southern Italians were more likely to be characterized as criminals and were thought to be part of the *mafia*, Italian organized crime. Both the North and South participated in *vendetta*, or retribution, if a family member was killed.

To be frank, each part of Italy thought it was better than the other part. Northerners looked down on Southern Italians, as Americans did later, based on stereotypes. They felt themselves superior and didn't try to hide their prejudice. Northern Italians were viewed as capitalists, snobbish, and elitist by Southerners.

Cultural Foodways

Another obvious difference in the cultures of the two regions was food. The climate of Northern Italy supported the growth of rice and corn in the Po River area so *risotto and polenta, a corn-based dish* were among the favorite staples In the South, however, more wheat was grown. This lent itself to making pasta and pizza. The North had more room for dairy cows and cattle so butter and cheese were used in traditional Northern cooking. In the South, olive oil was used to make traditional dishes. Spanish conquerors brought the tomato from the New World and introduced this versatile vegetable to all of Italy.

Folklorists, anthropologists, and more recently, sociologists, have long studied cultural influences. The term, "cultural foodways," refers to behaviors that influence what people eat. Foodways, in a given culture, define what foods are acceptable— e.g. cattle meat vs. horse. Donna Gabaccia wrote about how ethic food became eventually merged in American cuisine. However, at one time being able to fix an esoteric ethnic food was part of an ethnic identity. [17]

This is why Americans tend to think of Italian food as basically food from the southern region of Italy due to the large numbers who came. Pizza, is typically Neapolitan or southern Italian. Eventually, pizza became part of the overall food industry. Some claim spaghetti with meatballs is an American dish; this may reflect the scarcity of meat the diet of the poor in Italy. American immigrants found that meat was an abundant food item in their new country; in Italy only the wealthy would have meat as a normal part of their diet.[18]

Gender and Migration

Overall, migration was overwhelmingly male. This was because men were considered the breadwinner of the family; the wheels of capitalism need cheap labor to move the new economy along. [19] The wives waited in Italy until their husbands decided to move the family to the United States. Often, women had to wait several years before being summoned by their husband.

Since Italian women were encouraged to be homebodies, it was frightening for them to travel to a strange country alone. Not speaking the language, nor having any idea of the geography of this New Land, made leaving the security of home even more challenging. Furthermore, migration meant saying goodbye to family and friends— except, of course, for those children who joined their mothers on the journey.

Fears Women Faced

Immigrant women faced many types of fears—fear of the ship and traveling across the ocean and fear of an unknown land and what awaited them there. They also regretted leaving family, friends, and country behind. Many of us might not realize the courage it took for our grandmothers to decide to migrate. Bianca de Carli, likely from Lombardia, sailed from Italy alone. She later wrote about how she felt upon arriving at Ellis Island:

> *" A thousand times a day during the last day or two I put my hands on my passport and papers, which I kept wrapped in a handkerchief. This was just to make sure they were still there. One of my companions said, 'Signora, you are very foolish! When you keep your hand inside your dress, you were telling everyone that your papers and money are there! Maybe a bad person will see. Take your hands away!' Now, years later, I know it was foolish and silly, but we heard so many stories about others who were turned back because of papers not in order…. No one trusted even their pockets because… crowded together most of the time on the ship; it would be easy to have our pockets picked.* [20]

Race and Prejudice

In the United States, any group with a different religion, skin-shade, language, or culture was viewed with suspicion and discriminated against. For example, Catholicism was viewed as dangerous by Protestants who believed that Catholics did not obey not elected politicians, but only the pope. It was also thought that Catholics did not share the same values and work ethic as Protestants.

In the early 1900s, The Dillingham Commission's pseudo-scientific classification of races divided Italians into two distinct races. Northern Italians, or "Alpine Caucasians," were tall and long-headed. In contrast, the Southern or "Mediterranean Race" was of short stature, dark, and long-headed. True, due to its position in the Mediterranean, Sicily has seen its share of many races and genetic diversity is part of its heritage. The commission goes on to claim that there are distinct personality differences among the "races."[21] Contemporary social scientists dispute the idea of racial qualities being inherent in different peoples. Race is understood differently today is more complex than simply skin or cultural differences and is no longer considered a sign of innate inferiority. Northern Italians tended to be lighter-skinned and more like their European counterparts, while Southerners, having mixed over the generations with invaders from around the Mediterranean and North African, were somewhat darker, or swarthy. Hence, Southern Italians faced greater discrimination both in Italy in the States.

Reception in the United States

Italians generally faced a hostile reception in the United States. Had President Lincoln not been assassinated in 1865, their fate might have been quite different. He had passed an act that supported immigration only a year before his assassination. However the act was repealed shortly after his death.[22] The second, and by far the greatest wave of immigrants from Italy, came between the 1890s and the 1920s, when restrictive immigration laws were passed by those who were unhappy with the quickly changing character of the American population. White Anglo-Saxon Protestants viewed the increasing number of Catholics and other non-Protestant groups as a threat to a cohesive national image. Among the anti-immigrant groups that came into being were the No Nothing Party and the Ku Klux Klan.

Some Returned Home

Not all immigrants stayed in the United States. Some returned to Italy with the money they earned and bought land—something they impossible had they remained in Italy. In addition the person could now boast of adventures in a strange land.[23]

CHAPTER 3

Iowa Coal

T o speak or write about black diamonds in a state like Iowa, one might suppose that the author was referring to Iowa's rich soil, rather than coal. Early settlers were interested in farming; coal was used as a way to heat their homes. *"The emergence of the coal industry helped remake the face of America."* The nation was transformed by this fuel source from rural and agricultural to urban and industrial. As coal was first available for local use in Iowa from "drift coal" (coal visible due to erosion), people did not have to do deep-shaft mining there until 1860.[24] The importance of coal soared when the Chicago, Rock Island and Pacific Railroad Company started laying tracks and began looking for sites close to coal mines. Seymour, near the southern border of Iowa, was one such location.

The Growing Need for Coal

In the 1880s, the nation was on the cusp of shifting from being an agricultural nation to an industrial one. Use of coal surpassed that of wood for heating homes, but later, petroleum surpassed coal for the premier spot in energy.[25] The Civil War boosted the prominence of the coal industry as coal was used for energy in the manufacture of arms and naval vessels. Coal was needed to power engines in the growing transportation industry of trains, ships, and steamboats. Soon the price of coal rose as did the number of new coal mines. The ethnic diversity of the United States increased as the need for workers from abroad grew tremendously. Entrepreneurs now saw this rock as valuable for more than just heating homes. Production continued year round as companies moved west to Iowa, Kansas, Colorado, and Wyoming. Coal production emerged in several major regions: Pennsylvania and Appalachia, known for anthracite coal, a harder type of coal that burned hotter and longer; the Midwest, West, Southwest, Rocky Mountains, and Pacific Coast, which yielded mostly lignite or bituminous, a softer coal.[26] By 1895, Pennsylvania, Illinois, Ohio, West Virginia, and Alabama produced close to 72% of the total U.S. coal tonnage[27]. Between 1892 -1925, about 12,000 to almost 20,000 workers labored in Iowa's coal mining industry. Most camps were in Central or Southern Iowa near the Missouri border. Dorothy Schwieder focused on Seymour in her writing because of the large number of Italians who had migrated there. She was able to aptly describe the efforts of Italian immigrant women to create decent lives for themselves and their families despite poverty and sub-standard housing. [28]

The British Model of Mining

In the United States, coal mining was modeled after the British method was common in the previous century. This was not surprising considering the sizable wave of British miners who had immigrated to the United States in search of work. In general, these British miners appreciated the need for unionization. They brought along their technical skills as craftsmen and a strong work ethic. They wanted shorter work hours, better pay, and improved working conditions in the coalfields of the United States.[29]

Although their ideas of reform did not win out, their technique of "room and pillar mining" soon became standard in the United States. If the coal seam permitted, workers would dig out a "room" and leave a pillar of coal in place to support the ceiling. Wood and dirt props were then added to strengthen the supports. This was known as "room and pillar mining." Excavated coal was loaded into carts and raised to the surface and weighed. Workers were paid for the amount of coal a man could process, rather than the number of hours spent underground. As Roy noted, If a miner had a good seam that was fairly thick, he could cut and load 3 ½ to 5 tons in a typical workday.

Union Gains

Before unions began to fight for better working conditions for coal miners, a 10-hour day was standard. Men often went underground before daybreak and didn't get out until after sunset. Literally, darkness was their lot. For illumination, they might have a candle or a lamp of sorts attached to their headgear. The mines were poorly ventilated. Wages were low. Any extra money the women were able to earn often went towards the education of their children. The workers quickly realized that the scant education provided by the company meant that their sons would wind up working in the mines by age 16—the youngest age at which a boy could be hired. (Of course, in dire situations, such as the death of the primary breadwinner, an even younger son would have to go to work in the mines.) Girls might be able to get a clerical job or become a teacher, although few such jobs were available in mining towns.

The situation for miners and their families changed for the better after 1905 when the United Mine Workers (UMW) became active in Iowa. After finally achieving an 8-hour workday for miners, the union began to concentrate on social issues such as better housing, death benefits, sanitation, better schools, and even a strike fund. Through the efforts of the UMW, the quality of life in mining camps gradually improved.[30]

19

Housing and the Company Store— *1895-1925*

Mining companies preferred that workers lived near the mines. This cut down on the amount of time it took to get to the mine and begin working. As most mines were in remote areas, it behooved the company to build housing nearby. Investing in quality housing did not make economic sense because a mine seam would generally run out within 10 years. The houses that were thrown up were cheap and uniform. Unfortunately, miners were required to pay rent on these decrepit places.

Given the remoteness of many of the mines, the mining companies would provide a store that sold food and other necessities. The goods in these stores were overpriced and the mine owners strongly frowned on anyone who shopped elsewhere.

How Coal Miners Were Viewed: Seasonal Work

Until the 1860s, coal mining was seasonal work. As coal was used for heating homes, it was essential in winter, but not in the summer. This often meant that miners and their families had to move on a semi-yearly basis. Many Italians in Iowa found summer jobs in nearby Chicago. Interviews indicated that they would often live with relatives. This constant moving around made miners appear to be unstable, shiftless, and prone to just pick up and leave.

Many mine operators had a negative view of their workers. When, in 1919, Professor Nichols of Iowa State University was asked by the state to investigate coal-camp housing, he was told by mine owners that *"the miners are as a class morally and mentally inferior to practically all other day laborers, and, therefore, [are not] entitled to the same standard of living. In addition, they would not appreciate better housing and not keep it up."*[31] Nichols and union organizers disputed this view. They found that workers were more than willing to maintain decent housing.

In the 1920s, the employment of foreign-born workers reached its peak. Northern European miners were seen as craftsmen due to knowledge and techniques acquired before emigration. Southern Europeans, however, were often seen as inferior because of their lack of language skills. Because their English was limited, they were not always quick to understand orders or to communicate with people of different ethnic backgrounds. As new mining machines became more common, machines replaced those who had strong backs, but lacked mining skills.

The second generation also faced difficulties. Edna Padovan remembered that, although she had been born in the U.S., she considered herself to be a foreigner, *"because my parents spoke a foreign language. The fact that you were born in this country did not make you an American. I knew it did technically, that I was as much of an American as anybody, and I'm ashamed to admit it, but I was ashamed to admit that I was Italian. In college, I felt that people looked down on Southern Europeans. If you were German or Swiss or Norwegian there was not that feeling. People would always call Italian 'wops' and 'dagos' and I think I was supersensitive and that it bothered me a lot"*[32].

Lola Nizzi recalled the prejudice she faced in college and in school. *"I recall, coal miners were looked on down on in general, as were Catholics and Italians. I felt we had three strikes against us already"*. [33] In elementary school, she too was called derogatory names by the children of local farmers.

Disasters

As the mining industry grew it was often poorly regulated, many disasters occurred in the early years of the industry. These accidents claimed the lives of many immigrants who were inexperienced at mining. During the 1800s, every major mining state experienced at least one major disaster. Iowa fortunately only had one fairly significant mining disaster. The "Lost Creek Disaster of 1902", occurred before many immigrants had arrived in Iowa. What occurred was a misfiring of a blast hole needed to make more coal available to dig. In this instance, miners re-used a hole in which a misfire had occurred. The resulting flames ignited the coal dust in the air, causing the death of 12 men; another eight were seriously injured. Two miners, Frank and Joseph, with the Italian surname, Gaspari, were among those killed. Both had wives and children and were possibly related. By April of the same year, a new state law was passed that specified that explosions could only be set off under the supervision of a competent miner.[34]

Hardships Women Faced in Iowa Mining Camps

Dorothy Schwieder showed, with unflinching reality, the many hardships faced by the first group of immigrant women to settle in Iowa. Most migrated from small, rural towns such as Fiumalbo, Frassinoro, and Riccovolto in the provinces of Emilia-Romagna and Liguria in Northern Italy. Today, Riccovolto is a village of only 23 people. Young people, seeking industrial jobs, move to cities like Bologna in what is now a wealthy region of Italy. As it was once a very poor agricultural area, peasants left in droves to seek a better life for themselves and their families in the Americas and Northern Europe. This sounds like a life of poverty the Sartore family had, which the women might have imagined they would to return to.[35]

Upon arrival in Iowa, women were disappointed to find that their new homes were flimsy shacks, built in flat, treeless fields. The women faced further frustrations when they learned that potable water was often not readily available in the camps. Where wells had been dug, they were often poorly sealed and a housewife might find a dead rodent floating in the drinking water. In addition, during the warm, rainy months, due to improper drainage, large puddles of water formed, creating the perfect breeding ground for swarms of mosquitoes. Another insect problem was bedbugs. Paulina Biondi said that these bugs were so rampant that her hands bled from trying to scrub them away. Other problems faced by the women included leaky roofs, sagging doors, and window frames that did not keep out the snow.

These and other issues were something the wives could put up with for a short period of time, but, as these conditions continued on, many women became frustrated and discouraged. Most thought that once enough money was saved, they would be able to return to Italy. Few, however, would ever go back to Italy—not even for a visit.

Taking in Boarders

Many first generation women did not have time for outdoor activities. Instead they had grueling daily routines. They had left similar workloads in Italy, like Lorenzo's mother, due to poverty. In Iowa, the women often took in boarders to supplement the low wages earned by their husbands. This meant that the women had to do extra washing, sewing, cooking, and baking. They often baked small, tasty items to put in the lunchbox of a boarder. Cookies were always a treat, as were pie and cakes. Some women got up at 4 AM to bake so the men would have something fresh to take in their lunch boxes. If there happened to be an Italian- speaking grocer around, a representative would visit the homes and take orders for food. This greatly benefited those women who had never learned English.

With all this extra work, did boarders bring in a great deal of money? The luxury system charged a flat eight dollars a month. In the economy system, the wife added up the weekly bills and divided that amount among all adult boarders. Not surprisingly, the economy system was preferred. Women with large families might keep two or three boarders. Those with fewer children to care for might have up to 14 men living in the house. Boarders were usually younger men for whom the women felt sympathy. Realizing that they were far away from home and had no wife to take care of them, the women tried their best to make them feel like part of the family.

Life in Town

Some families in Iowa were lucky enough to be able to purchase a home in a nearby town, such as Seymour. Although those who lived in towns had more opportunities than those who lived in mining camps, the women still had rigorous work routines. They had to tend to their gardens and fruit trees, can fruits and vegetables, milk the cows, churn milk into butter and cheese, and feed the chickens. Those with enough time and money you could raise a pig or two. Pigs would be butchered for fresh meat, salami, sausage, and head cheese[36].

Could You Take It?

In the mining camps of Iowa, there was no indoor plumbing. People had to fetch water in large buckets in order to wash. Men expected a warm bath after work and the women were expected to provide the bathwater.

Imagine yourself as a new bride from Italy used to walking to the fountain in the center of your city or town to get water for washing. In Iowa, you have to hike to the nearest river with a bucket, and, once the bucket is full, carry it back home. This process has to be repeated several times until there is enough water for bathing all the men in your household. If your shoulder begins to bother you, switch to the other arm and move the pad that you have made to ease the strain of carrying the bucket. Once at home, you have to heat the water on your stove until it boils.

For bathing has to be done on a daily basis. Laundry can sometimes be put off for a week. When washing clothes, you again have to boil water on the stove. As miners' clothes are encrusted with coal dust, you have to vigorously scrub each piece on a washboard. When you are finished with the men's laundry, you have to mend and iron the children's school clothes so that they will look respectable. If you have younger children, who cannot walk with you to the river, you have to find a way to keep them occupied or hope to find good neighbors with whom you can share childcare duties.

Your life is an endless round of washing, cleaning, cooking, and childcare. If you have enough room outside, you can plant a few vegetables or raise a few chickens. *The life of the wife of a poor Italian miner is a life of hard work and poverty. You, like many other women, will cry during your first months in Iowa, wanting to return to the familiar life you left behind. No, life in Italy was not easy, but at least you had family and friends who spoke your dialect with whom to share your tribulations.*

Experiences in the Camp

Mary Braida, aged 18 and a newlywed, soon found that there was not enough insulation in her home to keep out the cold of an Iowa winter. One night her husband put his work boots under the stove so they would be warm in the morning. The next day, when he got up to leave for work, the boots were frozen to the ground.

Angelina Argenta, who lived in the Big Jim Cole Camp in Wayne County in 1900, disliked the shack that they rented. She lamented that "the house was very poorly constructed so that snow blew in around the windows and covered the bed." The furniture was so dilapidated that her husband had to tie bed springs together with bailing wire. Upon learning that a return to Italy was not in her future, Angelina cried her entire first year in Iowa. [37]

Bruna Pieracci and her mother, Filomena, migrated from Emilia Romagna. Bruna noted that women found the *"mining camps as a major contrast to the mountain villages that they come from. The (Iowa) camps were very similar— clusters of small boxlike homes made of wood and painted gray or boxcar red."* Northern Italian women were used to stone homes that had been around for generations. Bruna stated that the flatness and uniformity of the mining camp area led the women to refer to the area as "The Sahara."

Some women were never able to cope with the harsh realities of life in a mining camp. Filomena Pieracci was one of them. Bruna relates that her mother was extremely homesick for Italy and spent her time dreaming of the day she would return to her homeland. Filomena basically shut down and left Bruna to run the household. As Bruna's father spent most of his life underground in the coal mine, it was up to Bruna to become "the heart of the family." Filomena was never able to return to her beloved country. Upon her death, a packet of soil from home was placed in her hand.[38]

A new bride, like Paulina Biondi, did not have the luxury of a honeymoon period to get acclimated to the new culture and environment. Although she was still getting acquainted with her husband, it was an arranged marriage, she was obligated (out of economic necessity) to board up to four bachelors. The only privacy the new couple had was a burlap curtain hung between their bedroom and the bedrooms where the boarders slept. This young woman was only 17 when she arrived in Iowa, yet she managed to raise a family of five and keep no less than four boarders at all times. The Bondis rented a four-room company house. Although this was not ideal, it was better than living in a cramped three-room home. For a period of time, the miners had different shifts which meant that some were home during the day, and others at night. When asked if she would be willing to live like this again, she swiftly replied, *"If I had my life to do over again, no men around the house, no men around the house. No out!"*[39]

Paulina also recalled that after she had just given birth to twins, the camp well ran dry. The only well with water was the one for the company boarding house. As it was locked, Paulina took an ax and smashed the well lock. In her mind, the health of her newborn children was paramount.

Comradery

Despite many problems and challenges (and perhaps *because* of them!), miners stuck together. Father Gorman, one of the priests who visited the camps (miners could not attend mass as there were no Catholic churches nearby and miners had no means of transportation), observed, *"If someone died, some other family took over the children. Everyone helped everyone else."* A foster family would not officially "adopt" a child, but would give the child a home until he or she was old enough to work. A widow might need extra help because losing a husband meant losing the primary wage earner. Often a widow would move in with relatives and do jobs like taking in laundry in order to support her children.

Medical Care

Medical facilities were standard in many mining camps, however, in Iowa, no formal medical facilities were available. Instead, the company would contract a local doctor to provide services for employees and their families. The monthly fee for this service was taken out of a miner's pay. (Miners were allowed to pay on an installment plan if money was short.)

Although these doctors could help deliver a baby, some women preferred the help of a midwife. In the coal camps with no local doctor under contract, midwives often served as health care advisors to pregnant women. Skilled midwives could bring in a small amount in payment for their services. However, if a mother was a family member or close friend, there would be no charge to deliver the baby. Giacomina Cambruzzi, a midwife from Fozano, Italy, brought her birthing skills with her to Iowa. Giacomina took it upon herself to visit a new mother twice a day for two weeks until the mother was on her feet again. After giving birth, a woman was expected to rest for the first nine days. Of course, many women did not have this luxury!

A Woman's Limited Social Life

The social world of Italian immigrant women was limited and entertainment was infrequent. Some women remembered with fondness the Saturday night "kitchen dances." With one or two men playing the accordion or violin, couples would dance the evening away! These dances often provided opportunity for second generation daughters to meet a prospective spouse. (Of course, these girls wanted to marry a fellow Italian!) Another form of social interaction for the women was the knitting circle—a custom the women had enjoyed in Italy. The women gathered to knit socks and other warm garments that the cold Iowa winters required. At the same time, they often played "matchmaker" for the young girl seeking a spouse!

The Social Boss

A "social boss" would be the first person a newly arrived miner would go to for help in finding lodging or a wife. (The boss himself was a desirable spouse for second generation girls because of his social standing in the community.) The social boss handled many problems immigrants faced, including paying taxes or tickets. The boss also assisted miners with the chain migration of next of kin from Italy. Victor Cambruzzi, like most social bosses in Iowa, was bilingual and bicultural. His wife, Giacomina, helped find newcomers a place to board.[40].

Hope!!

While most of us, having other options, would not want to live in a mining camp, it was for many of the first-generation women an improvement over the lives they had lived in Italy. Despite the heavy workload and less than optimal living conditions, Paulina Biondi found life in Iowa fulfilling. She, and other women in the mining camps, realized that their time-honored roles as wives and mothers gave meaning and purpose to their lives. They felt that, in the United States, unlike in the old country, life did not have to remain the same generation after generation. A person could imagine a better life down the road. The presence of hope made many of the hardships worthwhile!

CHAPTER 4

Thurber— A Texas Coal Town

Coal in Texas? Certainly the Lone Star state stands out for its many unique features, but for oil, not coal. A century ago, however, it was indeed known for deposits of the valuable rock. Between 1880 and 1921, Thurber, located in West Central Texas, about 75 miles west of Ft. Worth, was the largest coal company mining town in Texas. It was also one of the largest producers of bituminous coal in the state. Thurber was a company town owned by the Texas and Pacific Coal Co., which in 1918 became Texas Pacific Coal and Oil.[41] Coal mining in Thurber was closely linked to railroad demands and railroads were essential to the growing economy of Texas after the Civil War. Texas needed commercial transportation in areas where there were no rivers for boat transportation.

Thurber was well-known for its conglomerate of nationalities. At one time it was probably the most ethnically diverse community in the state

Of the 18 different nationalities in Thurber, Italians made up about 52% of coal miners (although Italians made up only 25% of the total population), followed by the Polish with 12%, the Mexicans with 11%, and other Europeans 9%.[42] The rest of the miners were American born, including some African Americans. By 1910, over 500 Italians worked in its mines.

Working Conditions of a Thurber Coal Miner

The life of a coal miner in Thurber was often referred to as a "hellishly hard job." Lorenzo Sartore explained that *"men had to work from a prone position [due to narrow seams of coal; their average output was 2 ½ tons of coal a day. Coal dust covered the miners from head to foot. The dust... fouled the local air, and caused many to become sick with black lung. Sometimes [dust caused explosions] and cave-ins killed workers. A dear friend of mine lost both of his legs when someone carelessly lit a keg of blasting powder. He had a wife and two young children"*[43].

Elliott Lord noted that ..."*workers rose at 4 AM, ate breakfast and prepared for work. Then they left for the mines. The mines might be as far as 3 to 6 miles from the village but in the mornings and evenings miners were taken to work and back by two special trains.*"[44]

"Exploitationville"[45]

Thurber was an exceptionally exploitative company town, as were many other coal towns. Miners were paid low wages for extremely dangerous work. All 900 acres of Thurber were surrounded by barbed wire. Guards were posted at the gates, monitoring those who came in or went out. By taking such measures, the company owners prevented union recruiters and peddlers (who wanted to undersell the company store) from entering and hindered workers with cash from making purchases off site. Michel Foucault would have labeled Thurber as a *"panopticon"*— a term he used to describe "an area under constant surveillance by those in power in order to exert social control." [46] Despite the constant observation of who entered and exited the compound, one housewife, whose family owned a horse and wagon, managed to shop elsewhere and hide purchases under her long skirts. The goods she bought had to be unloaded under cover of darkness!

Miners were paid in "scrip"—a kind of paper money or coin that could be used only in the mining camp; this practice was common in other mining camps. This forced miners to purchase all goods (at greatly inflated prices!) from the company store. As rent and other company services, such as health-care and water, were deducted from workers earnings, miners frequently ran out of scrip before the end of the month. Of course, the company allowed miners to place items on their tab, which immediately placed them in debt to the company. Tennessee Ernie Ford's 1955 hit song, written by Merle Travis "Sixteen Tons," poignantly captures the plight of coal miners with the words, *"I owe my soul to the company store."*

Unions and Thurber

The owners' greatest fear was union organizers. Struggles between union representatives and profit-oriented companies were often heated or violent. "Few other American businessmen were as anti-union as the coal operators." [47] For a while Thurber was known as a nonunion town. Thurber company officials claimed that their stores were simply meant to be convenient for the workers and their families. The miners thought otherwise. Furthermore, miners viewed the barbed wire enclosure as a "devils device" to ensure a lucrative monopoly for the company. [48]

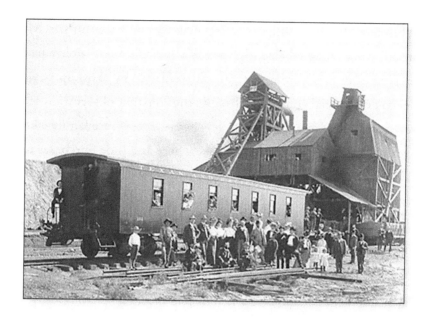

Italian miners are credited with helping Thurber become a town rather than just a camp. They also led the unionization of the mines. As it was impossible to do union business within the confines of Thurber, union members found ways to meet in the nearby town of Strawn. Among the first fourteen people to join the union in 1903, three had Italian names—Peter Grosso, Gior Guiseppe, and John Rollando. The main organizer for the United Mine Workers (UMW) was Joe Finiglio, a Piemontese, who got a job as a miner in Thurber. (He of course, risked beating or even death if the company found him inside.) [49] Joe was able to persuade many of his fellow Italians to join the union. In 1903, the United Mine Workers held an effective strike. The miners' wives, hopeful that a strike would lead to a better life, supported union measures.

During a union drive more than a thousand workers signed up on the Labor Day 1903. When their families were evicted from their homes and their husbands were terminated by the mining company, women dutifully packed up their belongings and moved on. While most families went to a nearby tent camp provided by the union, others sought jobs elsewhere in the United States.[50] Still others returned to their homeland. In the tent city, the women did their best to make both their husbands and their children feel at home. They encouraged the children to play and scraped together meals with the meager provisions provided by the union. Women had another positive influence on the striking miners. Due to their strong presence, excessive drinking was curtailed and there were no drunken brawls with strikebreakers. The strike ended peacefully, the United Mine Workers of America were granted the pay increase and an eight hour day paying the workers bimonthly, 26 working days would be considered a month and so dues would be collected for the union when the men got paid. In addition, the union would pay the wages of the weight checker who recorded the amount of coal dug. The miners held out for over three months and the company finally gave in to union demands. At a time when unions often excluded foreign workers, the Thurber strike showed how a united racial alliance could work to accomplish union goals. Thurber went from being notorious as a nonunion town to the most unionized town in the nation! The strike of 1903 resulted in higher wages, a union check weigh man (responsible for weighing coal and determining the amount due a miner), and the removal of the despised barbed wire fence. One of the owners allegedly said "you boys now own the mine". Three years later, in 1906, at Mine #7, Frank Vittoria led a protest by Italian miners which resulted in the granting of a second UMW Local, "The Italian Local." Lawrence Santi and Lee Americo, both bilingual, were state legislative representatives for the Italian Local.

In Texas, in 1917, oil supplanted coal. Liquid gold was struck in Ranger, a town near Thurber. The two towns were close enough that some executives living on New York Hill in Thurber could commute to work in Ranger by car. As production in Thurber slowed, workers tried another strike, hoping for an increase in their pay rate. Unfortunately, the company firmly stated that in light of the dwindling need for coal, they could not afford to raise wages. Workers again moved to a nearby tent city. Soon, however, seeing the sharp decline in the need for coal, they gave up and moved from Texas to coal mining camps in places such as Illinois where there was still steady work in the coal industry.

Housing

The owners of the Texas and Pacific Coal Company built a permanent camp around the new coal mines. Hundreds of houses were rapidly built. Schools were also constructed and doctors were brought in to give care to company employees and their families. The goal was to make Thurber "a place you wouldn't want to leave."

At first houses were small and basic. Planning was minimal. Most were T- or L-shaped. Often the back door of one house opened onto the front door of another. Most were little more than "a roof over your head." Built from wood, it even the roofs had wooden shingles a picket fence surrounded each home and then back was the outhouse.[51] Eventually the company began to build larger and nicer homes. Unlike yards in the Iowa camps, many yards in Thurber were rocky and not suitable for planting a garden. Houses were painted either red, gray or yellow with cheap paint that quickly wore off, resulting in weather-beaten, drab-looking houses. Eventually, water was supplied to homes after the company built two lakes to hold water. Unfortunately, the price per barrel was inordinately high. Despite Thurber's large brick factory that produced bricks from local clay, most streets were unpaved. Italians lived on the north side of Hill #3 and Polish families were on the south side.

The Work of Women in Thurber

Gino Sartore noted that women's work in the mining camps was often over-looked.[52] The truth was that the women worked just as hard as the men. The same as in Iowa, to supplement a miner's meager pay, women took in boarders. For $18 a month, a miner was given a bunk bed, two daily meals, and a work lunch. Laundry service was also included. One woman took in 18 boarders, possibly over a period of time, while caring for three children of her own. Because family was important in Italian culture, the women tried their best to make young, homesick Italian miners feel like part of the family. The tasty Italian dishes that the women prepared helped ease the miners' nostalgia for the homeland.

Women made a significant contribution to family income as they pre-pared food, cooked, cleaned, did the laundry, sewed items of clothing, and sold items such as dairy products and garden produce to outsiders. It is important to note that the income of the women tended to be steady, while that of a miner often was not. If a miner was unemployed for a period of time, the earnings of the wife helped support the family. Although it was not possible to own land in Thurber (as all the land was company-owned), many Italians bought land just north of the town in Thurber Junction. Numerous Italians opened businesses there: Santi Drug Store and Paper Route, Peretti's Ice and Garage, Auda Grocery, Taramino Picture Show and Dance Hall, Vietti Meat Market. The industrious Italian women of Thurber often found work in these establishments, further adding to the income of their families.

Memories of Victor Lucadello's Mother Maria as told to Leo Bielinski in Thurber[53]

Domeni and Maria Lucadello's first home, House #120, was on not on "Italian Hill," but near downtown. It was a good place to live because it had four rooms and not many houses nearby. The neighborhood was a mixture of Italians, Polish, Mexicans, and Irish people. Victor remarked that Italian Hill was like a "Little Italy" that could be seen in St. Louis. Unfortunately, besides being called "Italian Hill," it was also known as "Dago Hill."

What Victor's father appreciated most about #120 was the size of land, about 3 acres of fenced land. It had a barn, chicken coop, and a pen for pigs. Near the pigpen were the family outhouse and the wash shed where Victor's mother would wash clothes and his father would wash the coal dust off his body after work. Eventually, at the request of the union, the company put in washing facilities for the workers at the mines.

In one corner of the kitchen was the icebox. A large cooking stove was at the other end of the room. His parent's bedroom was near the kitchen and Victor and his sisters, Maria and Neta, shared a nearby bedroom. The other room was used to store food: crackers for the children, flour, sugar, and cornmeal to make polenta. Eventually the family moved to the east side of town in an area that later became known as "Lucadello's Valley."

Victor recalled that his mother was very thrifty. She would use dandelions in salads and boil the tough leaves with other vegetables. Not even the dandelion roots went to waste! His mother roasted the roots to make a drink similar to coffee. She would sing many Italian songs as she did her outside chores. She boiled water on the outdoor fireplace to do the laundry. She scrubbed the dirty clothes, rinsed them, and hung them out to dry. She also sang while she made bread outside. She even sang as she peddled her sewing machine. During hunting season, she sang as she dressed the wild game caught by her husband.

Music and Color

Italians were remembered as both musical and colorful! Thurber was also known as a musical city. Not only would Italian wives sing as they did their daily chores, the sound of music pervaded the town as accomplished musicians, such as Bart Bertino and Dan Raffael were brought in. The Italians jammed the Thurber Opera House to hear classic operas performed by touring troupes. There were several bands in the town which would play gigs in nearby towns. Not only did the Italians have a band, but their band would often travel around Texas to perform. Each year, at least a dozen concerts were given by different groups at open-air pavilions. At the Italian Pavilion in Thurber, known as "The Bearcat," everybody would listen to the music and dance.

On social occasions, (even at funerals!) the women wore long, colorful skirts that almost touched the ground. These skirts were made of fine fabrics, such as velvet, silk, and taffeta and were elaborately trimmed with lace or other ornamental touches. Women also wore jewelry such as crosses, earrings, pendants, necklaces, or even velvet ribbons that they brought out only on special occasions. Their colorful beauty was in sharp contrast to the bleak surroundings of a coal mining town! Men tended to dress more conservatively. They wore dark suits made of fabrics, such as corduroy, with little or no extra trimming. [54]

A Wedding

Rita Buffo Stoddard recalled the wedding of her older sister:

"At my sister's wedding, the feast lasted several days. The band was hired to play for dancing on the first day; from then on an accordion player was hired to play for the singing and dancing. It was customary among these Northern Italians to have rice as a special dish for weddings. This rice was called <u>risotto</u>, and it was special indeed. At a large wedding, the rice would be cooked in a large washtub. Into the rice, the women poured gallons of chicken broth, chicken giblets, tomato sauce, and pounds of Italian grated cheese. A salad, a great variety of meats, and a very special barrel of wine would be served along with the rice dish. All that wine was available and there was always a favorite drink, beer. As the kegs emptied during the wedding celebration, they were stacked on top of each other to look like a pyramid." [55]

Memories of Mauro Toniutti: A Great Grandson's Tribute to His Family

Unfortunately, for the purposes of this book we have few histories of women preserved. One story of an immigrant woman was chronicled by her great grandson, Mauro Toniutti, almost 100 years later. Mauro retraced the steps of his great grandparents their journey to Thurber (see di Anamaria Bianchi on line, in Italian). [56]

He begins the story on June 3, 1903 when his great grandparents, Giovanni and Caterina Toniutti, disembarked from the ship that had brought them from Europe to New York harbor. The *Kronprinz Wilweim* had departed from Germany with a cargo of men and women—and their hopes. The ship's passengers were carrying cardboard suitcases, hemp bags, and other necessary items. They had a little money in their pockets. Women wore handkerchiefs and long skirts. Their dark eyes were deep set from the long journey. Among the passengers were two people from the small town of Carnia, in the province of Udine, in the modern Italian region of Friuli-Venezia Gulia. Caterina, a young bride about 26 years old, was ready to start a family with the 33-year-old Giovanni. At that time, it was very difficult to advance in the world—for a young couple, it was even more difficult. As they descended on crowded Ellis Island, they were both eager and fearful of the life that awaited them in the land they believed to be "El Dorado." On this immense new continent, there would be room for all of them! The unknown future had a strong appeal. They hoped they would be fortunate in this new land. Mauro asks the reader to imagine how these immigrants must have felt as they fled hunger, extreme poverty, and backbreaking work.

Mauro says that he had no idea know what caused his great grandparents to select Thurber. Thurber was not the usual destination for most European immigrants. He speculates that they probably had some acquaintances who told them about this mining town in the heart of Texas. [1]

After arriving in New York, it took the couple over a month to travel to Texas. Giovanni was certain he could find work in a mine. In Thurber, the couple moved into one of the wooden shacks that were lined up in regular rows. In this little home, the Toniutti family grew. Their eldest son was Mauro's grandfather, Disdero. Next were Isolena and Virgil. Their two youngest children died early. Ribello died at 11 months old from pneumonia, while Dauphine died at 6 months of cholera. In a time of high infant mortality, due to poor hygienic conditions and poor knowledge of medicine, to have two children die was not unusual; however, the loss of a child is always a blow to a family.

In an aside, Mauro raises several questions about medical care and wonders if doctors were just too expensive or if there was little sanitation

---

[1] Gentry, 127, supported this notion.

available. According to the well-known historian of Thurber, Mary Jane Gentry, for $0.50 a month a miner could pay for healthcare and a doctor. She does not mention whether or not this healthcare included family members.[57][2] Since in other mining camps the family was included, it seems reasonable to suppose that this was the case.

When the grief-stricken Caterina asked the doctor why her child had died, he replied, "The air of this place is not suitable for the Italians." Mauro speculates that these words settled like stones in the hearts of parents, adding to the pain of the loss of their little ones and planting in them the fear that the coal-dust-ridden air really could harm Italians. Because of their concern for their own health and that of their other children, and because of their homesickness for the "green of Italy," they made the decision to return to their homeland.

The couple had hoped to return home with stories of Texas and their American-made wealth. Instead, they returned with the sad story of the loss of their children. Perhaps they were haunted by the thought that, had they stayed, they might have been able to actually live out their "American dream" of wealth and prosperity. Upon their return they became known as the *Americani*. The names of their two children and their death are recorded on a special plaque in the Thurber Cemetery, according to Bielinski.[58]

---

[2] In Arizona in 1903, an alliance between Mexican and Italian workers also proved fruitful. Similarly, in Colorado, American workers in Northern Colorado caved in to company pressure, while immigrant workers in Southern Colorado held out and were successful in getting the company to acquiesce to union demands. Union representatives, and even the famous 19th century labor activist, Mother Jones, praised the "alliance of foreigners" which courageously and successfully stood up against unfair labor practices.

The End of an Era

By 1933, Thurber was being dismantled and moved away, brick by brick and house by house. From the almost 1000 Italians in Thurber at one time, recently there were only four Italian descendants remaining in nearby Thurber Junction/Mingus . The only visible evidence of a past Italian presence in Thurber was the bocce ball courts at New York Hill. Today it is difficult to imagine why anyone would leave family and friends to migrate to a strange country to work under such harsh conditions. There was, however, opportunity in Thurber— something that was totally lacking in many impoverished European countries at the time. I'll let Victor Lucadello have the final words about Thurber: [59]

> *"The last days of my youth, were also the last days of the town of our birth; a haven for the Italian immigrants and other immigrants who came to coal town of Thurber at the turn-of-the-century"*

Copper comes next as we shift to the Upper Peninsula of Michigan, or U. P. as it is often called, where a quite different type of company town is found.

CHAPTER 5

Copper Country—Michigan's Upper Peninsula

H as anyone ever said to you, "That place is out in the middle of nowhere"? That is an accurate description of the location of the Upper Peninsula of Michigan. Where is it?

It is above Michigan's mitten-shaped peninsula and is bordered by Lake Superior to the north and by Lake Huron and Lake Michigan to the south.

It is attached to the upper Northeastern corner of Wisconsin. The U.P. area became eventually attached to the state of Michigan as an "unwanted step-child," in the 1820s. This was only after a Michigan territorial judge led a movement to create a new, distinct Wisconsin territory, citing the distance between the U.P. and Michigan's territorial capital, Detroit. At the time, people already living in Michigan were not a particularly interested in the U. P. They regarded the peninsula as part of Wisconsin. However, when the Erie Canal was finished in 1825, the number of Michigan settlements soared and interest in the territory began to grow.

For the Upper Peninsula to officially become part of Michigan, a vote by the federal government was needed. Unfortunately, a snag occurred because the "Toledo Strip," a piece of land on the Ohio-Michigan border, was surveyed incorrectly. This strip of land ideally would have become part of the new state of Michigan. However, in the election year of 1836, the already powerful state of Ohio ignored Michigan's demands and dismissed any legal claim the state of Michigan had on this land. Ohio proceeded to name and claimed the Toledo Strip for itself. The territorial delegate to Congress made a suggestion that more land in the Western Upper Peninsula be given to Michigan as compensation for losing the Toledo Strip to Ohio. Moreover, it was implied that the U. P. could be valuable to Michigan because of its iron ore, natural copper, and other resources. (The 4000-pound Ontongagon Copper Boulder— now in the Smithsonian Institution—was proof of the mineral wealth of the U.P.)[60] Eventually, Congress decided to attach the entire Upper Peninsula to the new state of Michigan. This didn't set well with the people already living in Michigan because they didn't want to have admission into the union delayed for this "frost-bit connection." In the end, the Upper Peninsula was given to Michigan and finalized in 1837 by President Andrew Jackson. Michigan became the 26th state of the United States on January 26, 1837. [61]

Early Uses for Copper

It was probably the Paleo-Indians who first found a use for copper in Michigan. They were hunters—and game was abundant around 4000 b c e. They most likely used the copper available on the surface rather than digging mines. They pounded the copper into shapes to make spear or arrow heads. In 1843, the first copper mining boom in the United States began in the copper deposits of the Keweenaw Peninsula—a small peninsula in the northwestern region of the U.P. The area that deserved the title of "Copper Country" was in the western side of the U.P. centered in Houghton and Keweenaw Counties, although other areas try to claim that name. [62]The remoteness of the copper mines in Michigan was emphasized by Sara Rice. [63] She observed that Chicago is 420 miles from the peninsula and that even Detroit is 210 miles away. The area is 2000 miles from San Francisco, which was the largest Northern Italian settlement in the West at the time of the copper boom[64].

Mining in the Upper Peninsula

Most immigrants to the U.P. came from Northern Italy— 80 percent from the Canvese area of Piemonte north of Turino the capital city, 10 percent from Lucca in Tuscany, another 5 percent from Lombardia, and a small number from other provinces in the North. [65]The earliest Italians arrived in 1860 to mine in the Hancock area. They had jobs waiting for them in the mines and mills of Calumet & Hecla, Quincy, and several other mining companies. These companies were in desperate need of large numbers of low paid semi-skilled workers. The Calumet and Hecla Consolidated Copper Company was the most successful corporation to mine native copper in Michigan's Upper Peninsula. Through nearly a century of mining activity, the company produced in excess of 4.5 billion pounds of refined copper and issued over $200 million in shareholder dividends. Unlike many of its competitors along the Keweenaw Peninsula, Calumet and Hecla successfully expanded its operations over several separate mineral bodies, developed capital-intensive ancillary industrial facilities, explored diversified non-mining enterprises, and remained a significant mining corporation at the national and international level well past the district's most productive era.

Uses for copper during the Civil War

Copper alone was used to protect the hulls of ships from damage. Many widespread uses for copper emerge when it was made into a fusion. Tin and copper produced bronze while copper and zinc became brass. At the time many of the small firearms used in the war were composites of copper and zinc. Very popular at the time were brass bands used to rally troops as well as instill patriotism for either side. The instruments in a brass band were derived from tin and copper which yielded brass. The durability of copper in such a composite source provided buttons, belt buckles, and other items for Civil War buffs to find still intact.

Out of the Mines

At first, Italians were mostly given jobs that involved physical strength. It wasn't until later that some left mining to start their own businesses. Some went into "cooperative merchandising" — a method of business they adopted from the Finnish immigrants in the Upper Peninsula. According to Russell Magnaghi, corporatist saloon in Iron Mountain was able to sell beer at half the cost of other establishments in the area.

Other Italians in the U.P. were able to develop sophisticated business enterprises as early as 1898. One group of immigrants started the Italian Mutual Fire Insurance Company in Laurium. This company continued in business until 2020. It still appears on the internet as the Great Lakes Mutual Fire Insurance Company. Although the Upper Peninsula was not primarily an agricultural area, some Italians were able to make a living by using the farming skills they had learned in Europe. They grew enough extra food to sell the surplus. Their grape harvest would be turned into *grappa*, a potent liquor made by Italians.[66] Some farmers made money from bootlegging. One area known as "Dago Valley" was mostly dairy farms producing milk and asiago cheese. Not all Italians in the Upper Peninsula were from Northern Italy. Some Southern Italians crossed into the United States from Canada to dig a massive canal through the city of Sault St. Marie. Some immigrants from Naples found work on the railroad lines in Chippewa County and later in the charcoal-chemical plant in Marquette. In Hermansville, the IXL Lumber Company hired people from the region around Venice to work in their lumber yards. Within a few short years, Italians had made the transition from subsistence farming to manufacturing. Some Italians in Michigan eventually went to work for the Ford Motor Company.[67]

By 1910, there were around 10,000 Italians living in Copper Country. Immigrant businessmen ran saloons, grocery stores, and bakeries to serve the growing population. Still others worked as tailors, cobblers, monument carvers, toy makers, and pasta manufacturers.[68]

Radicals and Troublemakers

Although many Italians were at first categorized as unskilled laborers, they eventually became known for their radical labor ideas. In 1902, the

Workmen's Mutual Aid Society was formed to improve working conditions.[3] The Workers International Benefit Society was organized in Vulcan in Dickinson County in 1914. These organizations were able to give workers some sick and death benefits

Strikes

As in other parts of the United States, unrest, generated by labor movements, caused headaches for company owners. In 1887 and 1894, Italian railroad workers went on strike. A dispute over wages in the barn ranges caused a strike in 1856.In 1894 in the Iron Range, miners went on strike. A year later, there was a strike by miners in the Marquette Range. By far the biggest strike in UP was held from 1913 to1914 occurred in Copper Country. Miners wanted to have the Union Western Federation of Miners (WFM) recognized by mining companies, especially by C & H. The corporation did not give in to their demands except to the one to institute an eight hour day. Thousands of men did not work for eight months and some workers were ejected from their homes. A tragic event called "the Italian Hall Massacre" occurred at Christmas time. To cheer the workers up and their families, the WFM hosted a party at the local Italian Hall. When someone, unknown, shouted fire people rushed for the stairs; the only exit here was one that had doors that unfortunately only opened inward. Over 70 people including children died piled up on the stairs.[4] Many miners moved west to other copper communities to find work. The strikers were harassed by local law officials or businessmen. One Italian newspaper (established in 1896) favored the mining company and denigrated the union. In the end

---

[3] In 1936, the society's name was changed to the Workmen's Mutual Aid Society of St. Anthony of Padua.)

[4] Some claim the company had arranged for this by planting a person who would yell fire. Not everyone believes t

the company won out and workers technically got some demands, like an eight hour work day, but the major corporation C& H did not accept the union; the company began a gradual decline in employment opened up in Michigan's auto industry.[69] According to historian Larry Lankton C & H was determined to control the workforce using manipulation armed deputy guards or mass firings which occurred in 1908.[70]

Women in Company Housing

The initial mining settlement in the region in the 1860s and 1870s was almost entirely male and the area was full of bars and brothels; family women who were not part of the shady life were not yet present. This made for an extremely unstable workforce. Men were often injured in bar fights or stayed home from work due to hangovers. Moreover, a man, not fully sober, was a danger to himself and others in an underground setting.

The housing that was built by the company had family occupancy in mind. Company owners believed that, with adequate housing, men would marry, settle down, and raise a family and that the wild and reckless behavior which characterized the "Wild West life-style" would be curtailed. The bottom line mentality companies really made no profit from housing. If there were repairs and needed to made the company would not likely fix it. The renter was on the hook for repairs.

A typical miner's house, of which there were not many, in Copper Country, an exception was in Southern Range. The house was built upon a mine-rock foundation, called a "Trimountain house;" a mine and town of the same name were in nearby. As with most company housing, uniformity was what allowed the company to erect a large number of houses quickly and cheaply. Rice notes, the houses were painted either gray or boxcar red; the only way to tell where someone lived was by the color of the house. The houses usually had six rooms and individual bed rooms were off the central entrance. The building was covered with clapboard or wooden shingles. At the rear of the house was a "snow room" where men entering could take off his dirty mining gear and/or wet snow-covered clothing before entering the main house. There, children, who had been playing outside, could change into dry clothes or at least take off dirty shoes before going into the house. An outhouse in the back area served their needs while water most likely came from a local well. [71]

Winter in the Upper Peninsula could begin as early as October and last through the following spring. Heavy snow was, and still is, the norm in the U. P., 399 inches of snow was the record but in general over 200 inches of snow could fall and temperatures were below freezing almost every day. Teresa Zana Harris recalled that when she was a child, the snow was so deep that her father had to shovel upwards to be able to get out of the house! [72]

At times, those with no one to shovel the heavy snow were trapped in their homes until someone with a shovel arrived. In the mid-1880s, shipping on the Great Lakes had to be suspended due to ice, closing off an important route of commerce. The environment was harsh and mining companies often had a hard time keeping workers, especially those unaccustomed to such extreme weather conditions. Fortunately, as most of the Italian miners in the U.P. had come from Northern Italy, another northern European group was the Finnish, so the snow of Copper Country was no novelty. They were used to cold winters and out houses! To keep warm during the long winter months, families would burn wooden slabs sold by lumber companies in the area. These wooden slabs came pre-cut—-just the right size for stoves. This saved both time and energy for the miners. C & H also allowed workers to cut firewood from the surrounding forests. Laborers often used a *fouchette*, with a sharp blade that folded up somewhat like a pocket knife. Many Italians households had their *own fouchette* and preferred it to an axe.[73]

What more could a worker ask for than a snug, warm house that kept out the cold of winter? Tyrolean workers might ask, "Who owns the patch of land on which this house has been built"? The answer was that all the land belongs to the C & H Company; a worker could rent the house but not buy the land, or lease land from the company but not buy it. The company also owned the local town—and this included churches and stores. In many ways, the mining company practiced a modern version of feudalism in which social and economic power was concentrated in the corporate owners and those close to them. Immigrants who dreamed of owning their own land had to move elsewhere.

Raising Crops and Animals

Unlike the drab houses in Iowa and Texas, during spring and summer, the Michigan homes were often encompassed by beautiful flower beds; one family was able to move into the flower business. Many residents also had fenced vegetable gardens. Sometimes these gardens were set in terraces, reminiscent of terraced gardens in Italy. Almost everyone had vegetables to eat. The most common foods grown were cabbage, beans, celery, tomatoes, zucchini, and carrots. The women canned many of the vegetables for winter.

Some families also raised chickens, and, if they had a room, a cow. Sara Rice notes that Maria Zanna always had a few chickens since they didn't require any special diet, but would eat whatever scraps were thrown out for them. If an unexpected guest arrived at dinner time, Maria would grab a chicken from the yard, cut out its tongue, and hang it upside down so it would die quickly. Victoria Bono said that most chickens in the area were called 'silver champions' because their feathers were silver from head to breast." Eggs were not only a good source of protein, but could be traded to neighbors for other necessary food items.

The women cooked traditional dishes from their region in Piemonte for their husbands, boarders, and families. One traditional appetizer from Piemonte was a dish called "*bagna cauda*" or "hot bath" in English. The dish was rich with garlic and heated oil; and was used to dip cold vegetables, breadsticks, or any kind of hearty Italian bread. Having a home-cooked, traditional meal was one way the women helped to make a strange land seem more like home. However, just as the tongue of immigrants had to become accustomed to a new language, so the palate of immigrants had to adjust to the food ways of a new society.

Preparations for Winter

According to Sara Rice it was a woman's responsibility to make sausage. Since pigs were expensive, two families often got together to buy one. Sausage was usually made in the fall so that the family would have something substantial to eat during the winter. Although the sausage was made at home, a butcher might be asked to supply the sausage casing. The process took several days. First, the garlic used was soaked in wine overnight. Then, a pint of wine was mixed into about 50 pounds of seasoned ground pork. The casings were filled with the sausage mixture and hung up to dry for three or four weeks. Then, alternating layers of sausage and lard were put in a 30 gallon crock which was placed in the basement for the winter.

Girls fishing for dinner

Gathering berries was a special treat as the women could get out of the house, have the companionship of other women, get good exercise and fresh air, and still feel that their activities contributed to the well-being of the family! Fish also added a welcomed diversity to their menus; both women and their children became adept anglers.

Women in front of a Trimountain House (South Range)

Immigrants Become Citizens

The Calumet and Hecla Mining Company was not only feudalistic, but paternalistic toward its workers. Company owners believed that it was their role to make solid American citizens out of these "foreign people." Immigrants also saw the desirability of becoming American citizens and the government encouraged immigrants to assimilate into the larger society. The Italian Citizen League helped immigrants fit into American communities and the Mutual Aid Group, formed in 1915, encouraged citizenship education .[74] Teachers were expected to enroll in assimilation and naturalization programs so that they could, in turn, teach others. Italians were involved in politics, offering to drive those who wanted to vote to the polls. In 1875, an Italian immigrant, Michael Borgo, was elected to serve on the first Calumet Village Council. After that, at least one Italian was on the Council until 1906.

Recreation and Cultural Retention

Although Italian immigrants wanted to be assimilated into their new culture, they valued their native language. Several newspapers and a literary journal were published in Italian. Also, until the 1930s, immigrants could take out books in Italian from the local public library. In 1889, miners in Calumet formed their own band. Other local Italian bands soon followed. The Italian Dramatic Group performed regularly at a local high school in 1928. Those nostalgic for home could even find Italian puppet shows—put on by the puppet-makers themselves. In addition railroads that ran mainly on Sundays went to two different recreational parks. One was Electric Park and the other was Freda Park. Once automobiles came popular, the train service was stopped.

People of Italian descent also participated in many different sports on the Peninsula—as athletes, coaches, or spectators. C & H also took steps to ensure that workers were entertained. Men could participate in any number of sports, recreation, and leisure activities, including bocce ball, billiards, cricket, ice skating, watersports, fishing, and hunting. [75]

Women's Work and Influence

According to Sarah Rice, 2002, "*The Italian women who came to Michigan between 1870-1920 brought with them a unique cultural identity that influenced their participation and attitudes towards home, work, recreation, and leisure activities, which, although altered by subsequent generations, still remains deeply embedded in Italian American women today.*"

In the early years of these copper mining settlements, women did not work outside the home since there were not a lot of jobs available in a mining town. Most women stayed at home raising their families and adding extra income by taking in boarders or by selling, wine, dairy products, or eggs. Women shunned prostitution and it would be very unlikely for even a widow to seek income by working in a house of ill-repute. Most likely a woman's family would somehow take her in even if they had very little themselves.

Christina Menghini did longitudinal research on Italian women in the Upper Peninsula of Michigan and their occupations. She found that in 1870, there were no women working outside the home. By 1900, however, the census showed 43 women working outside the home. (Taking in boarders, no matter how much work it involved, was not counted as "work" in the census. Most likely, at the time, working within the home was simply considered to be part of a woman's role as a wife.) Many of the jobs held by women in 1900 could be considered to be part of their gender roles. Five women kept boarding houses and five worked within a boarding house. Other jobs held by women at the time included: four saleswomen, three dressmakers, one *milner* (hat maker), two ran grocery stores, and one was a washer woman.[76]

Perhaps she could find work outside of the home, usually in a family owned business. At age 13, Victoria Bono began delivering milk for her father during the summer. Margaret Gardetto and her daughter, Mary, ran a grocery store while Mr. Gardetto worked in the mines. Filomena Giorgetti of Hancock helped her husband operate the Lavorini Macaroni Factory. After he died, she started her own food delivery service, specializing in pasta. Catherine Marta helped her husband in their bakery and when he died in 1909, she continued to run the business. In 1947, she was honored for having the longest operating bakery in the United States.[77]

Ten years later, in the census of 1910, 16 women headed boarding houses. By the 1920 census, more Italian women were working outside the home. One hundred forty six women worked as sales clerks in stores.

Others were dressmakers, nurses, cooks, midwives or ran their own business Unfortunately, Menghini did not specify whether or not these were immigrant women or second generation women. (I suspect that many of the women working outside the home were second generation women who could both read and write in English.)

Grocery Shopping

The women, of course, were expected to shop for food. Two local Italian grocers took care of Italian speaking customers. To take the grocery orders, the grocers' clerks went house to house (on opposite days so the two stores didn't have to compete with each other). The clerks spoke Italian and would explain to the women what was on sale that week. The clerks carried ledgers in which to write down the orders. The women had small pads on which they wrote down what they had ordered, so that when the items arrived, they could be checked off.

Boarding Houses

According to Sara Rice's interview of Catherine Fausone Opal who said, "everyone had boarders." Nerce Ciabitari, whose husband, Angelo, worked as a rock houseman at the Franklin Mine near Hancock, took care of 21 people—her relatives and 11 boarders. Katherine Meinardi Zanotti migrated to the United States with her husband, Domenico, but the couple planned to return to Italy within a few years. Katherine did not just take in boarders, she actually ran a boarding house, and, as was the case with many Italian women who took in boarders, all her boarders were either relatives or came from her village in Italy. (Taking in complete strangers was frowned upon.) Katherine cooked, cleaned, and did laundry for all her boarders. In addition, she did sewing for herself and her granddaughter.[78] Katherine was listed in the 1900 census as "proprietor of a boarding house." This was unusual since taking care of men was considered part of a woman's social role, and, women who had boarders were seldom noted in a census. A year after Domenico returned to Italy, Katherine gave up her dream of easy wealth in Michigan, and joined her husband.

Sewing

Katherine Meinardi Zanotti only sewed for her immediate family, while her daughter-in-law, Catherine Vincenti Zanotti, was skilled enough to make it her living by sewing. Catherine Vincenti Zanotti was an excellent seamstress. She had learned to sew at young age and soon began making clothing for the Italian women of Houghton County. When customers came to her house, she measured them for dresses in her living room or kitchen. She personally delivered the clothes to the homes of her clients.

Religious Involvement

In the town of Calumet, Catholic women would spend what little leisure time they had at church or involved in church activities. Calumet and Hecla provided land and building materials to any denomination that wanted to build a church on their land. At first, Italians went to the any nearby Catholic Church or to the French Catholic Church, but soon found that they lacked influence within these churches. Also, many of the practices in these churches were different from what they were used to in Italy. The Italian community decided to request a church of their own, and, in 1897, St. Mary's Church was built. The company gave them land and $2000 to build the church. The first mass was celebrated in August 1897 on the

Feast of the Assumption of the Virgin Mary. Some 2000 people attended the ceremonies, including a bishop and leaders from non-Italian Catholic organizations. Members of the Christopher Columbus Society came in carriages following the high-mass blessing of the cornerstone of the church. Those who did not live in Calumet were unable to attend a totally Italian church. The towns of South Range and Atlantic Mine shared a priest who came on alternate Sundays to say mass.

(Photo Sara Rice collection)

Not all Italians were Catholic. In the 1880s, Waldensian missionaries, from an organization based in Chicago, went to Iron Mountain to minister to Italian immigrants. Other Italians joined the local Presbyterian Church, which had established a mission in the U.P. in 1907 to serve immigrants from Italy. Their community center in Caspian was very popular with immigrants.[79]

Women's Organizations

These women of Upper Michigan were really ahead of their time. In 1902 in the town of South Range, the Daughters of Italy was founded. Jennie Coppo remembered that *"a group of women walked to the mountain on a really stormy day to sign up women for membership. Before the day was over, 100 women had enrolled as members."* The organization provided sick benefits for $0.50 per day. A maximum of $50 would be paid out for an illness. Recurring illnesses were not covered. The death benefit was $100, with an additional $10 for flowers and for masses to be said for the deceased's soul. The women borrowed the format for their meetings from the rules of men's organizations (which, of course, the women were not allowed to join). It wasn't until 1930 that women were allowed into the Sons of Italy. In 2017, the national organization officially became the Sons and Daughters of Italy! [80]

In Calumet, the Ladies Aid Society (affiliated with St. Mary's Church) was organized in 1897. In 1917, the Daughters of the Eternal City formed. It began with 20 members and grew steadily. In various locations, lodges of the Lady Druids cropped up. By the 1930s, almost every Italian community had at least one women's club. These associations gave women the opportunity to meet with other women of similar backgrounds and experiences. They could talk and play cards. Through these social and religious organizations, women were exposed to the world outside their own homes. Many women developed skills in leadership and gained influence in the community. [81]

Sara Rice contends that *"the women faced opposition from their husbands when trying to organize lodges or benevolent societies."* The men believed that a woman's place was in the home and not out and about attending meetings. Despite this opposition from their husbands, the women were not deterred from organizing these associations. Rice notes that such organizations *"enabled women to develop a sense of power and belonging and an opportunity to socialize away from home."*

It was not only women who had clubs. Men also established mutual aid societies, such as the Italian Mutual Society of Calumet, which was formed in 1875. Through these organizations, for a small monthly fee, immigrants could get both health and death benefits. As the first generation of immigrants died off, however, so did the clubs. By 2001, only three chapters of the *"paisano clubs"* were still around.[82]

Russell Magnaghi, 2001, [83] sums up life for Italian immigrants when he says that *"life for the Italian immigrant was not easy. Yes, America was a land of opportunity, but wages were low, and life was radically different from what they were used to. Many survived the acculturation process through clubs, friendships, organizations, and the aid of their children. It is known that many went back to Italy or turned to alcohol to numb the pain."*

Of course, Italians in the Upper Peninsula, as in other parts of the States, had to overcome culture shock and discrimination. As fascism began to rise in parts of Europe, so did problems for Italians immigrants. Mussolini, who became the fascist dictator of Italy in 1925, tarnished the reputation of Italians and it was unwise for Italians to be openly pro-Mussolini in the United States. Italian immigrants had to work even harder to be accepted in their new land. [84]

The next chapter deals with the mining community of Globe, Arizona. Although unions in the area had gained many advantages for the miners before most Italian immigrants had settled in the region, the immigrants still faced many challenges as they sought to become part of a new and strange community.

CHAPTER 6

Globe, Arizona

The city of Globe is in the Pinal ("pine-covered") Mountains of Arizona, about 87 miles east of Phoenix. Early explorers went to the area searching for mineral wealth. The quest took off in full force after the Civil War when troops, finally freed from their war-time duties, became available to aid adventurers looking for gold, silver, and other valuable minerals. General Crook began an all-out violent attack on the Apache people living in the area. Many were driven to reservations, one of which is near Globe (The San Carlos Reservation). As the Apache were no longer a major threat, adventurers were free to launch expeditions to seek their fortune.

From Silver to Copper

Early Mexican explorers thought there were large amounts of silver to be mined in the Pinals due to a 3-pound silver nugget of 90% fine silver found in the area. Although some gained substantial fortunes in the Arizona silver industry, not all were so lucky. Harsh living conditions, no available stores in which to buy supplies, harassment by outlaws, and renewed attacks on mining camps by Apache who left the reservation, proved discouraging. Although silver mining had played out by the end of the 1880s, copper kept mining interests around. By 1884, the Old Dominion Mine, or O. D., put

Globe on the map as a permanent city when it began to produce copper. O.D. remained the main mine in Globe for many years.

The city site was laid out in 1876.[85] To be called a city, one writer opined, it needed a newspaper and by 1878, Globe began publishing one, *The Arizona Silver Belt*. The city, however, still lacked amenities such as decent housing (many residents lived in tents), paved streets, and organized waste removal. Despite a boom in housing, it wasn't until 1906 that a sewer system was finally built[86].

Although Globe initially labeled itself as a 'white man's town," it was never as exclusive as Bisbee, a mining town in Southeastern Arizona . Globe lacked Bisbee's sundown law that mandated that all Chinese people leave town at dusk or risk death. Yes, the Chinese were allowed in Globe, but not to take jobs from miners as some feared, but to grow crops and to run small businesses such as restaurants and laundries. The Chinese residents of Globe were segregated and lived in a separate section of town. Mexicans tended to live in Ruiz Canyon, just south of Globe; some also lived on Euclid Street. However, in general, Globe was a very diverse city, especially when compared with Arizona's cattle towns, commercial centers, and other mining towns. In 1909 the town of nearby Miami, where low grade copper was mined, was established near Globe. Unlike Globe, Miami began with provisions for a police force, electric lighting, and a sewer system. About the time of Miami's inception, a new county, Gila, was formed with Globe as its capital.

Transmigration

Not all Italians came directly from Italy to Arizona. Some had lived in other areas of the United States, but, upon learning of the great mineral wealth in the Western states, had decided to head west. As Anna Giardino, a character in Dorothy Bryant's semi-auto biographic novel, stated, "*Home is, the world is, a cabin on a muddy road up the hill to a mine, is called Illinois, Colorado, Utah, and Montana. We moved, but it was always the same cabin, road, mine. We moved, but we moved west.*" [87] In fact, Dorothy's family finally settled in San Francisco, California. There was no place further west to go to look for fortune.

Some Globe residents also started their sojourn further west in the United States. Merced Beluzzi, her husband, Bartemelo, and their daughter, Angelita, had begun their American adventure in California. They later moved to Arizona, becoming one of the earliest Italian families to settle in the Globe area. Their names are recorded in the Arizona 1882 Territorial Census.

Cultural Capital

Pierre Bourdieu believed that in order to establish oneself in a strange culture one must have an idea of what is valued in that culture and of the status to which one can hope to aspire. There were many enterprising Italians who arrived in the Globe area who had this sense of how to achieve in a new and different culture. Pasquale Nigro acquired such experience or "cultural capital" -[88]-i.e. "living in a different culture long enough to know how some of the major systems work." He was born in Italy in 1845 and became a naturalized U.S. citizen shortly after arriving in California in 1871. He eventually became the owner of a successful saloon in Globe. Alfred Rabogliatti, from Piemonte, gained cultural capital in New Orleans, according to his grandson with the same name.[89] When he arrived in Globe, he immediately saw business opportunities. Since the local copper mines were growing rapidly, he recognized the need for adequate housing for the miners. Mr. Rabogliatti built a boarding house which was open to people of all nationalities. (At that time, there were few Italian women in the vicinity to provide this service.) He also opened the Wedge Saloon and built bocce ball courts behind the building.

What's in a Label ?

Outsiders often view ethnic neighborhoods, or enclaves, with suspicion. It may appear that the residents of such neighborhoods are "clannish" and just want to be with "their own kind." However, when ethnic enclaves are viewed from the perspective of social science, it becomes clear that these ethnic groups are living near each other because of poverty, discrimination, and linguistic and/or cultural barriers. Many of these newcomers might attempt to assimilate into the larger culture, but they want to do so without losing their own cultural identity.

Canyon Salé

The Italian neighborhood on Globe's Euclid Street, on the west side of the railroad tracks, was settled by people from the Canavese area of Piemonte. The Piemontese called it "Canyon Salé." (Italians referred to Euclid Street as a "canyon" because of its steep incline.) This part of Globe was also known as "United Nations Canyon" as so many of its residents were foreign-born. Unfortunately, another name for Euclid Street was "Wop Alley"— a pejorative term used in order to create social distance between the Anglo-Saxon and "foreign" population. (Terms like wop, dago, guinea, etc., give a sense of superiority to those using such terms.) If one checks early city directories, it becomes clear that the area was never totally Italian. It was mostly working-class families, including Mexican Americans who could afford only modest homes and enough land for a garden.

In this neighborhood, Italians socialized with each other as they worked on projects such as winemaking and beer production. In a sense, this area within Globe was like a "Little Italy" since many of the local residents owned stores or services geared toward other Italian immigrants. Women did not need to master English to be able to go shopping for food at Ernesta and Bert Vidano's Grocery Store on Broadway Street that carried cornmeal, polenta, and other items used in traditional dishes. The neighborhood, like many other Italian areas, was filled with music. Many of the locals could play instruments, such as the accordion, violin, or guitar, and had a substantial repertoire of Italian tunes. On a warm summer evening, an impromptu concert might begin on a back porch. Storytelling was another enjoyable pastime. Storytellers like Ricco Troglia, told tales while sitting in front of the Martinbianco Grocery on Euclid. Often storytellers would "serialize" the stories to keep their audience coming back night after night.[1]

Panama, Globe

Upon driving into Globe from the Phoenix area, one would first encounter a small Italian community referred to as "Panama" by Italians. Many families living there had also come from the Canavese area of Piemonte, from villages that were only about 10 miles from each other. This secondary area of Italian settlement informally got its name because many of the men who lived there had previously worked on the Panama Canal according to those interviewed. When that project came to an end, many of the workers moved north to the United States and settled in the mining town of Globe. (Not all came directly to the mining town; some had traveled a bit before settling on Globe.)

Union Gains in Globe

In the towns already discussed, miners lived in company housing and were unable to own their own houses and property. In Globe, however, due to union successes, when asked, "Who owns this land?", a miner could proudly answer, "I do!" Also, in most of the mining communities mentioned in this book, it was common for the wives of the miners to take in boarders in order to supplement the husband's income. This was less common in Globe. Because of union gains, the husbands of the women in Globe had decent wages and benefits as early as 1902 and Italian women were not as pressured to bring in extra income from boarders. Married women might take in boarders in times of financial stress or if they became widowed. When Kate Bigondo's husband died, she took 12 boarders into the small house where she and her four children lived. The work was so heavy that at one point she hired a cook and a young girl to serve meals!

Photo of Boarding House, Globe, AZ

Most men worked at the Old Dominion mine, or O.D. In the 1890s, the O. D. was purchased by a corporation based in New York. The new owners soon got into a conflict with the union over hiring Mexican workers. In 1895, in an effort to lower overhead, all wages were cut to the level of Mexican wages. Union workers immediately pressured the mine owners to fire alien Mexicans—i.e. all those who were not American citizens. The union came out victorious, and, as the local union began to thrive, decent, well-paying underground jobs became available for Italians. Although it was not typical for unions to accept new immigrants into their membership, an exception was made because local unions were struggling to get enough members to pressure companies into acquiescing to their demands. Throughout Arizona acceptance of Italians varied according to the local micro-culture. In some towns, like Bisbee, their wages were below that of their white counterparts.

Earlier miners saw themselves as having more mining skills than the newcomers and felt that their own wages should be higher. Therefore, they were against allowing newcomers into the union. In 1903, when the miners in Thurber, Texas walked off the job rather than capitulate to the company, Italian saloon owners in Globe advertised their support of the union's actions. Union leaders began to recognize that they needed to incorporate immigrants into the union. Eventually, Globe's union became a powerful force among Western miners. Perhaps its early success made leaders cautious about becoming affiliated with the more radical Industrial Workers of the World or Wobblies as they were sometimes called. Rather than affiliating with a group that was definitely anti-corporate, the union grew in terms of reputation by including members of ethnic minorities as a way to increase their power. The future of unions was to be multi-cultural in the modern sense of inclusivity rather than being divided into separate racial and ethnic categories.

The women of Globe could thank the stalwart women of Thurber for quietly packing up their belongings and following their husbands into a temporary camp. What happened in Thurber showed the WFM that ethnic groups could indeed work together and produce results.

Out of the Mines

Ironically, it was union membership that eventually allowed Italian miners to leave mining, with its unsafe working conditions, to pursue other occupations. Many Italians became the proud owners of saloons or grocery stores. Because of union victories, the sons of miners, unlike their fathers, did not have to settle for low-paying, dangerous jobs that required little skill. Through education, which had been strongly advocated by the unions, the next generation was able to move up in the world.

Italians immigrants were more likely than those from other countries to leave mining to open their own businesses. *"In fact only the Italian showed a predilection for any specific work other than mining, and that was the liquor trades, where they owned saloons and tended bar."*[90] In order to open a saloon, person only needed a knowledge of popular local spirits, a trusted friend to serve the liquor (and, if needed, to break up fights), and a lot of endurance to oversee the evening.

As these Italian owned businesses grew and prospered, jobs in family restaurants, stores, and laundries became available to Italian women. This gave the women of Globe work opportunities not available in most of the mining communities discussed in this book.

Conditions in the Mines

Two of the most common reasons for leaving mining were being unhappy underground and/or working under a foreman who constantly demanded that the miner work faster. A description of the interior of the work place at O. D. comes from Alice Hamilton, a physician who investigated health problems related to mining. It was 1919 when she *"stepped into a cage which was a type of flimsy, shaky elevator not having walls or anything you can hold onto which dropped down into darkness…some 800 feet. I trudged along, stooping to avoid overhangs."* [91] She actually had to crawl forward on hands and knees and then climb down an 80 foot ladder into the black pit. For her, the worst part of her experience in the mine was *"crossing deep pits on rails which were so far apart I felt sure I could fall between them if I slipped."* All the while she was down in the mine; she could hear the constant drilling of jackhammers. Her ordeal convinced her that the vibrations caused by the drilling were dangerous to the health of workers. Another threat to miners in the O. D. was the dust produced by these jackhammers. Many miners died from tuberculosis. Hamilton found that local doctors simply ignored these problems. Miners who left eventually moved on to work in the copper mines of Butte, Montana informed their fellow miners back in Globe that the Butte mines were "killer mines"—mines to be avoided if at all possible.

Women's Lives: Euclid Street:

Anna Troglia Faletti Interviewed by PCM 1981 in Globe, AZ

She put down her occupation as retired laundress when I interviewed her. At age 6 , she came to Arizona with her mother, Maddalena Revello Giacoma , to meet her father, Anton Troglia, for the first time. Anna had been conceived when Anton went home to find a spouse and the couple had married. In the States, just before Maddalena was about to give birth for the second time, Anton left for the copper mines of Montana. He did not return to Globe until he was dying. In the intervening years, he never sent money to the family. Although the Giacoma family lived nearby, and would help Maddalena out when they could, she was basically was on her own financially and had to take in laundry in order to make ends meet. Even though it did not in any way excuse Anton's behavior, he might have felt disillusioned by life in Globe. Anna mentioned that a lot of young Italian men came to the United States thinking they could shovel in money, however, all that was shoveled was dirt in their grave! When Anna was old enough, she went to work in the local laundry. She worked there for the next 30 years. When I interviewed her, she mentioned that, because of working for so many years at the laundry, she suffers from "bad feet"!

In 1918, when Maddalena became ill with the Spanish flu, Anna and her brother stayed home to care for their mother. Anna was extremely disappointed that her relatives in Globe didn't come by when her mother was sick. Anna also remembered that when she was 12 years old, and was stricken with typhoid fever, her relatives would not even give her a ride to the county hospital. Maddalena later died of stomach problems. She had been too poor to pay for the surgery that might have saved her. After her mother's death, the Robogliatti family helped Anna out. Alfred Robogliatti, and his wife, Martha, even stood up for Anna at her modest wedding as she had neither father nor mother to do so. During World War I, the Zucco family, who owned a grocery, befriended Anna. They allowed her to pay on credit whenever money was tight.

The Troglia family also lived in Globe, but seldom helped out the family, since they were not wealthy either. Fortunately, some aid came through the Red Cross. Anna regretted not being able to translate better for her mother, who struggled with English, and had a hard time understanding the Red Cross lady with the 'big purse" who came and told her she had to find work. Anna herself found learning English difficult. As so many of her schoolmates spoke her dialect, she and her classmates would often converse almost exclusively in Italian.

When aged about 15 or 16, Anna became engaged to Pete Giacoletti. She was even given a wedding shower! Pete had rented them a house to show he was serious about getting married. Unfortunately, Pete's family opposed the marriage and had him abducted and put on a train to California where they had relatives. As you might imagine, this incident caused a great deal gossip. Maddalena took a bus to the Giacoletti home and told off all of Pete's brothers. Indeed, in such a small community, gossip, even if later proven false, is a powerful weapon to shame people and to curtail undesirable behavior.

Later, another young man became interested in Anna, but, as she admitted, she was "green as hell." She didn't know what to say to her beau. Fortunately, working at the laundry had helped her learn about sexual matters—something an Italian family would seldom discuss with children. Anna went on to marry another suitor, who, at the time, was in the Armed Forces. She was very proud of the photos she had of him in uniform! Anna's husband later worked at the Castle Dome Mine on Highway 60 as a contractor for Schwartz Lumber. He was a jack of all trades and could also make cement blocks for the mine.

One of Anna's big regrets was that her daughter didn't finish college. She had wanted both children a daughter and ason to earn college degrees, but neither one did. At the end of his life, Anna's father got sick and returned to Globe. Because of his behavior and lack of concern for his family during all the years of his absence, he was not welcomed back into the family. Anna seemed concerned with all the family photos, passports, and other memorabilia she had collected over the years. She wondered what would happen to these things when she died. She had a strong sense of the value of family history.

Women's Lives

Jeanette Carretto Bowling interview PCM 1981 in Globe, Az
Nicknames

Jeanette's father's name was Giovanni Baptista Carretto. In the United States, he became known as John A.B. Carretto, since he ran the Arizona Bakery. Another John in the area was nicknamed *volpe* or fox.

Peter Obero, in his book about Italian immigrants, discusses the importance of nicknames or *sopprannomi* for people who migrated from Italy. Quoting Barth Cunico who did extensive genealogical research on families from the town of Asiago and is mentioned in [92] Obero states that nicknames in Italy could derive from almost anything. Nicknames might come from a prominent physical feature, such as height; a unique behavioral trait, like being a liar; an interesting habit, like wearing baggy pants; an occupation; one's place of origin; a favorite food; or a past event in a person's life. In Italy, families often remained in the same town for generations. This resulted in large extended families. Nicknames were often used to distinguish one branch of the family from another or one individual from another with the same name. Offspring, who migrated to America, often had a hard time finding their relatives as they were unaware of their Italian nickname. Women were also given nicknames, but as they were less likely to be given the same name as men, and as they would gain a name upon getting married, this practice was less common for women in Italy.

Both Anna and Jeanette remembered the many good times they had growing up. Anna recalled some of the fun she had at the dances put on by the Italian community—using local musicians. Much of the time music was old fashioned— a waltz, a foxtrot, or some of the old country dances that were still around.

Women's Lives Panama

At these dances many young Italian Americans met prospective spouses— among them were Anna and Jeanette's parents, John A. B. Carretto. Jeanette remembered a band that would come and play in Panama in 1909. She also had fond memories of picnics at Wheatfields, an open space between Globe and Miami. (St. John's Day was one occasion for a picnic in Wheatfields.) Jeanette recalled that her father would break out his accordion, his first purchase upon arriving in Globe. Her uncle, however, was the one who knew all the Italian songs.

Another occasion for merriment was a baptism. The infant's family would get a barrel of beer and they would have, as Jeanette said, "a hell of a time." After church, the party would drive to Wheatfields for a big picnic of polenta and sausage. Of course, wine would also flow!

Nita Morello Brigante, Jeanette Carretto Bowling, daughter of John and Mary Carretto , grew up in Panama. Jeanette's grandfather came to Globe around the turn-of-the-century. Soon after arriving in Arizona, he sent for his bride to be, from Piemonte, and they were married shortly after she arrived. Jeanette recalled that many Italian men from Piemonte had the first name Giovanni or John in English. Perhaps this was because the patron saint of the area was St. John. The surname Carretto could be found throughout Italian settlements in Arizona. There were so many men named John, that to keep them all straight, the community gave them nicknames.

I interviewed Nita Brigante in 1981. Her father's name was Pasquale, but he was known as "Barney" in America. He had one saloon in Panama and another in uptown Globe. He also owned a grocery store and a bakery and the North Bowl Grocery Store in uptown on North Broad Street.

The family's migration pattern was typical. Her father came to the United States first. His five brothers soon followed. Barney's initial stop was Gallup, New Mexico, where he opened a grocery store and a saloon. He then sent for his younger brother. In 1898, Barney went to Globe, while the younger brother remained in Gallup. His older brother, **Dominic**, went to Mexico. In Globe, Barney invested in property— mostly older tracts of land in back of the homes of other Italians. Barney's wife, Theresa, was his childhood sweetheart. She was 33 when she came to Globe from Pratiglione, Canavese near Rivarollo.

Although Theresa had been educated in Italy, she never learned English. As she wanted Nita to have a good education, she sent her daughter to school. Nita's given name was Antoinette , but her family called her "Netta." Somehow her name got changed to "Nita" at school and the name stuck!

Nita's father died ays after returning from an extended trip to Italy. (Long trips back to the homeland were not uncommon.) In The *Arizona Silver Belt* (4/25/06) an article on his death appeared, extolling him as a wealthy and influential Italian resident of Globe. Besides owning property in Arizona, he also had property in Gallup, New Mexico; Cananea, Mexico; and Italy. He'd accomplished a lot in his 41 years! Many widows faced a difficult time of raising their children when the principal breadwinner died. Theresa was grateful that she and her three children were well-off financially. The newspaper reported Barney's overall wealth as $100,000. His brothers, however, quickly amended that figure down to $12,000.

Barney's funeral, reported in the same newspaper (ASB 5/3/1906), claimed that it was one of the largest *"ever held in Globe; every carriage and light vehicle was pressed into service."* The funeral cortege, which included a band playing a dirge, proceeded from the Morello residence on North Broad Street to the Holy Angels Catholic Church, where services were held, and then slowly wended its way to the cemetery. The article mentioned that the casket was very elaborate with a plush white and lilac lining, silver mountings, and *"anything that at that time was considered consistent with the solemn occasion."*[5]

Shortly after Barney's death, his older brother returned to Mexico. Another brother, Felix, remained in Globe. He was both Nita's uncle and her *padrin or* godfather and used to take her on outings. When his sister-in

---

[5] If you are interested in reading Italian folk tales, I would like to refer you to **Italo Calvino's Italian Folktales-** (published in 1956)—a compilation of over 200 Italian folktales from the 1870s to the 1950s. The tales were originally narrated by ordinary people, at times illiterate, often women. Some stories featured feminine protagonists such as: *"Angela Smiraglia, eighteen-year-old country girl"* or *"a certain Rosina, an old woman who makes hose",* or *"Agatuzza Messia, seventy-year-old seamstress of winter quilts."* Calvino writes, *"Since the folktale, regardless of its origin, tends to absorb something of the place where it is narrated – a landscape, a custom, a moral outlook, or else merely a very faint accent or flavor of that locality – the degree to which a tale is imbued with that Piemontese, Venetian, Tuscan, or Sicilian something is what led me to choose it"*

law, Theresa, sold the family saloon to the Vernettis and went to Italy, Felix took over some of the family's affairs. Unfortunately, however, Felix was a "ladies' man" and not good with finances. Warned by letter, of her brother-in-law's lack of financial responsibility, Theresa had to cut her trip short and return to Globe.

Globe Today

As of the 2020 census, the city of Globe contained a little over 7000 people. Due to the city's ethnic diversity—with a mixture of people of European descent, Hispanic people, African-Americans, Native Americans, and a small number of Asians— Globe has been designated as a "diverse area" by the United States Census Bureau

On N. Murphy Street, just up the hill from DeMarco's Italian Restaurant, is the main entrance to the **"Old Dominion Historic Mine Park."** Visitors to the park can walk on trails through old mining areas, view old mining artifacts, and discover more about the geology and mining history of Globe. There's even a mine-themed playground for the children! The park is a fitting tribute to the area's mining past.

CHAPTER 7

Conclusion

N ow it's time I need to ask myself, "Did I tell the stories of those unknown Italian immigrant women considered by some to be of little worth?" In reviewing the chapters, I would have to say that I think I did. Since I am half Northern Italian and half Southern Italian, I would like to think that I can represent both sides. Although I had previously read **Black Diamonds**, it was not until I went back and teased out the stories of immigrant women that I realized how difficult their lives really were. By the time I was growing up, my Sicilian grandmother was no longer newcomer to the United States. Sadly, I did not realize the treasure trove of stories that she held nor did I ask her to tell me about her childhood. I, like many readers of this book, was a novice in understanding the difficulties faced by women when they first came to America.

"The Heart of the Family"

I also came to the realization that these women were indeed "the heart of the family," since the men fulfilled their role as "head of the family" primarily through their economic support of their wives and children. At the time of these camps, miners worked from before sunup to after sunset and so many of the children only got to know their fathers later in life when they were no longer working. It was the women who raised the children and made a home for them. The women had an especially difficult time when they first came to the U.S. as many of them were not only newcomers to America, but to their marriage. Some had not even had time to get to know their husbands in Italy before traveling to the States. Others, who married a man who had come back to the village looking for spouse, may have had unrealistic expectations of what America would bring. They had no way of knowing that the man they were about to marry was not a "big shot" in the United States, but likely at the bottom of the social ladder.

The women came with expectations both of married life and of life in the New World and their husbands had certain expectations of the roles of women—a role the women were to fulfill without the support of family and friends in a strange land with a strange culture and language, and often, with a strange man, she only knew through letters.

In what ways were these women "the heart of the family?" Sometimes it was simply by being from Italy and bringing a slice of that culture to homes in places very unlike where they had been born and raised. The women spoke the dialect of their husbands and they cooked their husbands' favorite dishes, albeit with ingredients not exactly like those in Italy, giving their husbands "a taste of home." This was indeed "comfort food" for the hard-working miners! Home was also a place where a man could relax, and if he was so inclined, discuss his views on the local union proposals—a conversation that in another setting would get him expelled from both his job and housing. Those women, who made an effort to learn English, were often able to help their husbands when a conflict or dispute arose that required a knowledge of English. Women also provided legitimated sexual intimacy.

The women not only supported their husbands emotionally, but often financially as well. At times, the women who took on boarders were able to almost double the low salaries brought in by their husbands. Although taking on boarders was not listed in the census as "work," it was indeed labor that was backbreaking, time-consuming, and exhausting! Not all women were able to adjust to life in the United States. Just as a transplanted shrub may not thrive in new soil no matter how enriched, some women did not ever feel at home in their new environment. In the chapter on Iowa, I mentioned Filomena Pieracci, who just gave up and allowed her daughter, Bruna, to take over the household. Bruna said of her mother, "She remained a stranger in a strange land."[93] On the plains of Texas, a new invention—meant for keeping cattle out of farm fields and gardens and for keeping stray Longhorns from contaminating the bloodlines of champion cows being bred for their quality meat—was gaining in popularity. Italian women, who immigrated to Texas, had never seen, nor even heard of, barbed wire before coming to the States. In Thurber, however, they were surrounded by it. Although they came from farming areas in Italy, this type of wire fencing had not been invented until 1876 (Wikipedia accessed 2021). That the women of Thurber were known for their singing, is a testament to their ability to thrive even in the most challenging of circumstances! To be surrounded by barbed wire and to be under constant surveillance would have made it difficult to feel that the houses of Thurber could ever become "homes with a heart." However, the women did manage to establish a community on Hill #3. Despite their circumstances, the women sang bits of operas or popular songs, and, both those who sang and those who listened, had their spirits lifted. As the women and their husbands set out to enjoy performances at the local company-provided theater, they were trying to "make the best of a bad situation."

In comparison to women in Iowa and Texas, the women of Michigan had better living conditions with nicely built company houses that could withstand the cold winters of the U. P. This meant that, unlike the women in Iowa, the women of Michigan did not have to walk back and forth to the river, only to a nearby well in order to provide their families with water for bathing, cooking, and drinking. This cut down on their workload enormously! Nor did they find themselves burdened with the high cost of a barrel of water as in Texas.

Women in Michigan also kept boarders. This extra amount of work brought positive results for the company, as well as for the family. Because the women boarded single men, the company was spared the expense of providing meals and building bunkhouses for unmarried miners. The outside income brought in by the women augmented what the men were making. Donna Gabaccia (1998, 80) estimates that close to one half to one third of immigrant families took in boarders.

The women of these mining communities were aware that they lived on a patch of company-owned land and so were not able to just pick up and leave if the situation got dire. When unions presented the opportunity, however, the women were willing to pack up and move to what promised to be "greener pastures." After all, they had already proved their mettle by moving from Italy to a new world about which they had heard so many fantastic stories. The women of the Upper Peninsula also had to confront the reality that their husbands' work in Michigan was not as highly valued by the company as was the work of the miners in Montana. Pick up and move again? When the hammer of the company came down upon the workers, women were ready to start again if they had to. They must have reasoned that moving another time could not possibly be worse than the first terrible tearing away from family and their native land. They had already learned English to some extent as well as different dialects of Italian, depending on which group they were living close to. They would bring with them their knowledge of Italian foods, as well as tender reminders of home such as a statue of a favorite saint, a crucifix, faded photographs of family, or a painting of the little village they had left behind.

Perhaps they are hoping to find a town like Globe, Arizona where miners were paid decent wages and where miners could purchase their own land. It was only when I started writing about Globe that I realized that I not only wanted to describe the difficulties these women faced in these mining communities, but that I wanted to present their willingness to stand with the union when it held out the possibility of a better life—even when this meant packing up and moving. In some situations, the women actively helped strikers by bringing them food and water.

In Texas, the families moved into a tent city with almost no amenities. Who knows what these women told their children to convince them that it was more fun to play outside in the dust than to have a permanent home. I can only imagine some of these discussions: "Be brave for your father is working hard to get you a better future." or "No, we won't live here forever, we will move on to something better."

The one thing that gave these women hope was their belief that the United States offered them and their children the possibility of a better future. Rosa Cavallieri told her compatriots in Italy that, in the United States, the poor could talk to the wealthy. It was not like Italy where the two classes never interacted or seldom had contact with each other. True, immigrant women might not have been considered social equals, but some of "the scraping subservience of the poor" was no longer expected.

What I learned from writing this book

By writing this book, I wanted to emphasize three areas often neglected in books about Italian immigrant women: First, the lives of Northern Italian women have been almost completely ignored in the literature on immigrant women. This absence is something Sara Rice commented on extensively in her thesis. For the most part, it is Southern Italian women who are discussed. This, of course, is understandable since the number of Northern Italian immigrants to the United States was substantially smaller than the number of their Southern counterparts. When I was asked to do a literature review for this book, except for *Rosa*, I couldn't find anything on Northern Italian women. This book is homage to these women, who first ventured to the unknown, and not always welcoming, shores of the United States.

Second, until I did the research for this book, I had not fully realized the extent of the role unions in creating better lives for these Italian immigrants. In Globe, Arizona, Italians were of fortunate enough to get in on the ground floor of labor union activity. Because of union achievements, miners in Globe could purchase their own homes and property. Owning the land allowed them to have gardens and domesticated animals, such as cows, horses, and even a pig or two. They also brewed beer and wine. The frugal Italians used the space to grow items that were financially beneficial.

Women in Globe did not need to take in boarders since their husbands earned decent wages. Although taking in boarders was advantageous financially, it was physically and emotionally draining for women who often had four children of their own and up to 16 added adult boarders. In addition, boarders were not always affable. They could be a fussy clientele, expecting a great deal for the little rent that they paid; some were even pressured women for sexual intimacy. Although, unlike Thurber, Globe did not have an opera house or theater, immigrants were entertained by Italian musicians and storytellers, and, overall, their circumstances were preferable to those of other mining communities.

Third, I discovered that prejudice could be found in even the most remote mining town. Although Northern Italian immigrants were few in number, they did not escape the prejudice that other immigrants faced, as shown by Roediger.[94] In Iowa, second generation children understood enough English to be aware of the disdain with which they were viewed. In Michigan, the term "dago" was used to designate a valley where many of the farmers were from Italy. Even in Globe, Italians found themselves when living in a separate part of the town and in death in divided cemetery. Was this to keep them, even in the afterlife, apart from mainstream whites?

While I was viewing handwritten census records, I noticed that the officials making these records did not always check off, "White," but would write in the margin, "Other," since foreigners did not fit in any available category. Stitt, also mentioned this. David Roediger [95] noted that Italians fell into an "in-between group"— that is, not white, but clearly not people of color, such as African Americans. Mexican Americans fell into a unique category. On the one hand they had been present in mining areas often for several generations, but, not all been present when the United States claimed parts of the Southwest under the Treaty of Guadalupe Hidalgo. Like Italians, they too were often Catholic and seem through a lens of pre-existing prejudice and stereotypes. In some situations, Mexicans and Italians were in the same category.

Although early Italians faced prejudice and discrimination in "the new land of opportunity," the Italy that they left behind was not egalitarian. Poor peasants were used to being treated like dirt and things were not initially better for them in the United States. Yet these immigrants believed in the American ideal of freedom and equality and were not willing to give up hope on that vision. Italians eventually did edge into the "White category" and were able to gain many of the advantages of being considered white, despite prevailing stereotypes of being linked to criminal behavior. Before this could happen, their children, unfortunately, were forced to bear the brunt of discrimination and prejudice in school. As some of the young women in Iowa mentioned, there was awareness that they already had three strikes against them before they entered the classroom— being from Italy, being Catholic, and being poor. This is a topic, remaining prejudice and stereotypes that needs further exploration—perhaps in another book!

BASTA/FINITO
or in English
Stop/Finished

Index

List of Illustrations

Endnotes

1   Elizabeth Scott *Those of Little Note: Gender, Race, and Class in Historical Archaeology*. Tucson, University of Arizona press, 1994

2   Rosa Cavalieri,. Marie Hall Ets, ed (Minneapolis, University of Minnesota Press, 1970).

3   Andrew Roy, *A History of the Coal Miners of the United States*. Columbus, Ohio: J.L. Tauger. 1907

4   Andrew Roy of the Coal Miners. Cleveland: Robinson, Savage, 1876. New York. Fordham University press. 2007.

5   Bolognani, Bonifacio. *A Courageous People from the Dolomites: The Immigrants from Trentino on U.S.A. Trails*. (Trent, Italy edition and patronage of the autonomous province of Trent-Italy. 1981)

6   Instiruto Italiano di Cultura, *Facts About Italy 23, Women in Italy*, New York, N.Y. January 1972.

7   Gabbacia, Donna. *From the Other Side: Women, Gender & Immigrant Life in the U.S. 1820-1990* Bloomington and Indianapolis Indiana University Press. 15-16.

8   Illaria Serra. *The Value of Worthless Lives: Writing Italian American Immigrant Autobiographies*. New York. Fordham University Press. 2007.

9   Schwieder. Dorothy. *Black Diamonds: Life and Work in Iowa's Coal Mining Communities, 1895-1925*. Ames, Iowa State University Press. 1983.

10 Denis Mack Smith, *Italy: a Modern History*. Ann Arbor, MI. The University of Michigan Press. 1997.115-217

11 Gilmour, David. *The Pursuit of Italy: a history of a land, its regions, its people*. New York. Farrar, Strauss Giroux, 2011. 176-229.

12 Isabella, Maurizio. *"Nationality before liberty? Risorgimento Political Thought in a concept text Journal of Modern Italian Studies* 17 (5) 201.

13 Both of my father's parents; my grandparents, both maternal and paternal were from near Palermo.

14 Belinski, Leo. *The Thurber connection*. Gordon, Texas Thurber Historical Association.

15 Forester, 431.

16 Wikipedia accessed 2021.

17 Gabaccia, Donna: *Ethnic Food and the Making of America* (Cambridge, MA Harvard University Press, 2000)

18 Hasia Diner. *Hungering for America: Italian, Irish, & Jewish Food ways in the Age of Migration*. Cambridge. Harvard University Press. 2001. 20.;

19 John Bodnar *The Transplanted: a History of Immigrants in Urban America. Bloomington Indiana. Indiana University press. 1985. 1.*

20 Joy Hakim. *A history of the US. Reconstructing America. 1865-1890.* New York. Oxford University Press third edition. 1993. Third edition. Revised. 116.

21 https://library.harvard.edu/collections/ immigration-united-states-1789-1930

22 Silverman, Jason. *"Lincoln's Forgotten Act to Encourage Immigration,"* (Washington DC). President Lincoln's Cottage, 7/1/ 2016.

23 https://www.loc.gov/classroom-materials/immigration/italian/the-great-arrival/ accessed 2/2022.

24 Schwieder, Dorothy. *Black Diamonds: Life and Work in Iowa's Coal mining communities 1895-1925*. Ames. Iowa State University press 1983. 1-3.

25 Schwieder. 112

26 Warington Smyth. *Coal and coal Mining* (London. DrStrshan Co press. 1869. 87. Reprinted. Kissinger.

27 Schwieder, 111

28 Schweider, 112.

29 Andrew Roy. *A history of the coal miners of the United States.*

30 Schwieder, 148.

31 Schwieder, 145.

32 Schwieder, 104.

33 Schwieder, 105.

34 Phil Hoffman, 105, *"The Lost Creek Disaster"* The Palimpest, V26, #1, 1945 1-16 (Iowa Research Online).

35 Bielinski, *Leo The Thurber connection.* Gordon Texas Thurber Historical Association. 1999. 38-39.

36 Schwieder, 88.

37 Schwieder, 89.

38 Serra. 119.

39 Schwieder, 145.

40 Schwieder, 69.

41 Hooks, Michael Q. *"Thurber: A Unique Texas Community"* Panhandle Planes Historical Review 56. 1983. 1-17.

42 Hooks, 1

43 Belfiglio, Valentine J. *The Italian Experience in Texas: a Closer Look.* Eakin Press Press Tx, 1995. 99

44 Belfiglio, 113.

45 The term was coined by Hardy Green in his book. *The Company Town: the Industrial Edens and Satnnic Mills That Shaped the American Economy. Ch 3, 5p7-8*

46 *Michel Foucault Discipline and Punish: the Birth of the Prison.* MD Keymar, Second Vintage Books Edition, May 1995.

47 Green. *The Company Town.* 59.

48 Mary Jane Gentry. *The Birth of a Texas Ghost Town: Thurber, 1886-1933.* College Station. Texas A& M University Press. 2008. 71.

49 Bielinski, Leo. *The Thurber Connection.* Thurber Historical Association, Gordon, TX. 1999. 199.

50 Mary Jane Gentry, 69

51 Don Woodward *Black Diamonds! Black Gold!: The Saga of the of the of Texas Pacific Coal and Oil Company.* Lubbock, Texas. Texas Tech University Press. 1998. 37.

52 Bielinski,, Leo. 37-52.

53 Bielinski, Leo in *The Thurber Connection.* 1-25.

54 Belfiglio, 113.

55 Gentry 78

56 Also titled Destianizione *Thuber*

57 Ibid.

58 Bielinski. The Search for…Grave.. 139 and grandson's memoirs, cited above

59 Bielinski, 35.

60 Pantell, Hope, editor. "*The Story of The Ontonagon Copper Boulder*" Washington, D.C. Smithsonian Press . 1971

61 Magnaghi, Russell. *Upper Peninsula of Michigan: a History,* Marquette Mi, Heritage Press. 2017.

62 Magnaghi, R. 2017. 17.

63 Martinelli, Phylis Cancilla. *Undermining Race Ethnic Identities in Arizona Copper Camps, 1880-1920.* (Tucson University of Arizona Press. 172

64 Rice I realized that since I received her thesis as an attachment I did not have pagination.

65 Magnaghi, Russell. *Italians in Michigan* East Lansing. Michigan Michigan State University Press. 2001 22.

66 Oberto, Peter. *A History of the Italian Immigrants from the Seven Towns of the Asiago Plateau. In the region of the Vento in Italy on the Gogebic Iron Range of Michigan and Wisconsin from the 1890s to the 1950s.* Lulu self Publishing services 2016. Chapter 3. Farming, Gardening, and Grapes page 89-92

67 Magnaghi, 2001

68 Magnaghi, R. 22

69 Magnaghi, R. Upper Peninsula. 80

70 Lankton, Larry. *Cradle to grave: life, work, and death in the Lake Superior Copper Mines.* New York. Oxford University press. 1991. 202.

71 Kevin Musser collection accessed 6/2022

72 Rice, 2002

73 Rice, 2002

74 Magnaghi R. *Italians in Michigan.* East Lansing. Michigan State University Press .2001. 22

75 Magnaghi, R. 2001. 27.

76 Magnaghi, Christina *Examining patterns of Italian immigration to Michigan's Houghton County 1860 to 1930.* Master's thesis, Michigan Technological University, 2004.

77 Magnaghi, R. 2001. 28.

78 Magnaghi, 25, 2001

79 Magnaghi, 2001 26—9

80 Website Sons of Italy and Daughters accessed 2021.

81   Foucault, Michel, *Discipline and Punish: the Birth of the Prison* (Second Vintage Books Edition), May Keymar, 1995.

82   Magnaghi, *Italians in Michigan.*

83   Magnaghi, *Italians in Michigan. 29.*

84   Magnaghi, ibid

85   *Honor the Past..<u>Mold the Future</u>"* Gila County Centennal, (Tucson, 1976).

86   Stitt, Colleen.

87   Anna Bryant. *Miss Giardino*. Berkeley, Ca. 1978. Ata Books.5.

88   Martinelli, *Undermining Race 77.* University Of Arizona Press 1998.

89   Grandson, same name. Alfred Robaglatti, pcm 1982 In Globe.

90   Stitt, Colleen. *Fickle Friends: Copper and community,* Globe, AZ Ph Dissertation, Arizona State University, 1990

91   Hamilton, Alice. *Exploring the Dangerous Trades.* Boston. Little, Brown. 1942.

92   https://www.bing.com/barth.comcunio.

93   Serra. 119.

94   Roediger David *Colored White: Transcending the Racial Past.* Berkeley. University of California Press. 2002. 37

95   Martinelli Ibid

CPSIA information can be obtained
at www.ICGtesting.com
Printed in the USA
JSHW032336050123
35446JS00007B/79